Compulsion to Kill

By Stephen Challis

Compulsion To Kill

Compulsion To Kill

Forward by Robert M. Ekes, M.A.

When we hear of an atrocity such as a mass murder in a mall, or a theater, or of someone's murderous rampage against children in a school it affects us all. We recoil in shock, disbelief, horror, and with many questions. What exactly happened? How did it happen? How was it allowed to happen? And most importantly what can be done to stop it from happening again?

In my own 25 year career as a clinical mental health therapist and consultant I treated many children, adolescents, and adults. I have been struck by the level of aggression and violence displayed by some people and I made efforts to study and research the origins of such aggressive behavior. Some of the research findings seem like common sense yet I am frequently dismayed that they don't appear to be recognized or utilized.

Upon reading Compulsion to Kill I was gratified to see that Stephen Challis is also aware of the research that I had seen in my own reviews of the professional literature. He discusses the findings and their significance. Mr. Challis also presents much more valuable information that we need to know as we search for answers and for antidotes to shocking violence that we see in our headlines.

Stephen Challis is uniquely qualified to present the information to us. He resides in Kentucky, USA and he is very aware of the American concerns regarding violence and firearms.

Compulsion To Kill

He discusses some events that I am sure many of us were not even aware of.

Mr. Challis' 21-year career as a police officer in the United Kingdom gives him the perspective to tell us about incidents in Europe and elsewhere that we commonly are not aware off. He is aware of other countries' firearms policies and their results, which many of us do not know. His law enforcement career perhaps contributes to his accessible style of writing that is clear, concise, factual, logical and very readable.

This book examines a number of significant mass murder incidents through history both in this country and in other countries. It presents the facts on how much violence we do experience as a culture and how this has changed over time. It explores the professional thinking about the mental health issues, motivations, and the personality traits of those who perpetrate mass murder. It acknowledges the complexities of trying to address those mental health issues. Also discussed is the role of the media in the public's perception of these tragedies and of firearms. It discusses some of the effects that the media and entertainment can have on the perpetrators themselves.

The book presents and evaluates some of the efforts that have been made around the world to address the problem of gun violence. Included is a discussion of the rate of gun ownership in 169 different countries including the USA and how this correlates with incidents of gun homicide. Most importantly this book discusses things that can be done to address the risk of murderous violence. This is, after all, what we all want when we address this subject.

Compulsion To Kill

The information presented in this book is information that you need to know. As the political rhetoric escalates like it does after every horrific incident the same questions are asked: What will stop this? Is armed security or gun bans the answer? The discussion of gun violence is frequently a single pointed discussion about the guns and often not about the violence, which is after all what it is really all about. The discussions are often emotional and they are sometimes conducted without important relevant information.

In Compulsion to Kill the information that may be omitted by those who are promoting one or another viewpoint is available to you. This important book can help us understand and be productive participants in the discussion of how to keep ourselves and our loved ones safe from the atrocity of violence.

Robert M. Ekes, M.A., MSW, LCSW

Kentucky Licensed Clinical Social Worker

Winchester, Kentucky 2013

Compulsion To Kill

Compulsion To Kill

Dedication

Dedicated to the memory of the following victims of the mass shooting at Sandy Hook Elementary School Newtown, Connecticut on December 14th 2012.

Charlotte Bacon,	6 years
Daniel Barden,	7 years
Rachel Davino,	29 years
Olivia Engel,	6 years
Josephine Gay,	7 years
Ana M. Marquez-Greene,	6 years,
Dylan Hockley,	6 years
Dawn Hochsprung,	47 years
Madeleine F. Hsu,	6 years
Catherine V. Hubbard,	6 years
Chase Kowalski,	7 years
Jesse Lewis,	6 years
James Mattioli,	6 years
Grace McDonnell,	7 years
Anne Marie Murphy,	52 years
Emilie Parker,	6 years
Jack Pinto,	6 years
Noah Pozner,	6 years
Caroline Previdi,	6 years
Jessica Rekos,	6 years
Avielle Richman,	6 years
Lauren Rousseau,	30 years
Mary Sherlach,	56 years
Victoria Soto,	47 years
Benjamin Wheeler,	6 years
Allison N. Wyatt,	6 years

Compulsion To Kill

Compulsion To Kill

Authors Note;

As this book was completed the horrific events at the Sandy Hook Elementary School in Newton Connecticut were unfolding. A full account has not been included as Police investigations are still on going, it may be months or even years before we get a true picture if ever. However from the initial Police reports some facts have emerged. This killer used guns he did not own. He took them from his dead mother and used her car to get to the School where he carried out the assault.

As at Dunblane, his victims were children in the first and second grade. At the time of this writing not too much is known about Adam Lanza. He was reported to be addicted to violent video games, to be unpopular at school and may have had mental issues. It is far too soon to say if he fits the same psychological profile as the other subjects in this book.

No doubt everyone will have ideas as to how we proceed, as happened after Dunblane many are clamoring for more gun-laws and even an outright ban. But those same people have no credible response to how that keep guns from people who are lawbreakers.

Compulsion To Kill

Until we are prepared to protect our children while at school with real workable solutions, as opposed to Political rhetoric we will continue to have other Sandy Hooks. I have dedicated this book to the 26 victims of Sandy Hook Elementary school. December 14th 2012.

Compulsion To Kill

Table of Contents

Compulsion To Kill

Compulsion To Kill

Introduction

When there is a horrific incident in the country, or for that matter in the world where many lives are lost as a result of the seemingly mindless act of one or two individuals, there is inevitably an outcry that something must be done. If the killer or killers used a gun, then the clamor is for more gun control. If no guns were used in the killing then the demand for some another type of legislation is brought up. Blame usually falls to the school, the social status, or the lack of supervision of the perpetrator. We hear of warning signs, social conditions, and restrictions being ignored and it seems that the blame is usually leveled anywhere but at the perpetrator.

In fact the likeliest persons to commit these crimes, according to statistics, fall into one predictable group.

They're 95% male and 98% are black or white — not a big surprise since more than 87% of the population is made up of those two races. If the killers' profiles are all cut from the same cloth then why is it that their crimes are not? The best known or at least most lurid of the mass killers in recent history are Ted Bundy, Jeffrey Dahmer, Jared Loughner, and James Holmes. These are the archetypal serial murderers, the killers whose crimes defy comprehension. Their crimes often play out over decades.

Compulsion To Kill

In most cases, people who commit such murders are driven by a dark, often sexual pleasure, and while remorse is often associated with the acts, which may account for the long lapses that can occur between them, those twinges of conscience are quickly overcome by the impulse to kill again.

There appears to be a charge and a thrill associated with these murders which do not seem to be the case with a mass murderer who kills at once. Few people are in a position to observe a killer such as Jeffery Dahmer at work and survive to testify about it. But plenty of people present at shootings like those at Virginia Tech (2007), Columbine High School (1999), and Aurora (2012) did make it out alive. They were able to describe the killer's demeanor as the shooting was taking place. These accounts do not profile a person who's thrilled by, or even much enjoying, what he's doing.

Instead, survivors report a cold joylessness to the actions, something that in its own way is a lot harder to understand than the perverse pleasure of a serial killer. What makes mass murderers do it? Trying to find the much-looked-for snapping moment, that one inciting incident that pushes a killer over the edge, rarely gets you very far.

According to Dr. Michael Welner, an associate professor of psychiatry at New York University School of Medicine, "Snapping is a Misnomer."

Compulsion To Kill

These people plan to carry out a mass killing without any indication of when they will do it. Instead of snapping, imagine a cage that someone has the capacity to unhinge. They simply decide that today is the day.

Mass murder, in short, is not a random act. There are conditions that explain it. Psychosis, for one, a brain injury in an otherwise healthy person can lead to similar violence. Damage to the frontal region of the brain, which regulates what psychologists call the observing ego, or the limbic region, which controls violence, reflection, and defensive behavior, can shut down internal governors and trigger all manner of unregulated behavior. "Somebody who had damage to both regions would be a bad player for sure," says forensic psychiatrist Neil Kaye, a faculty member at Jefferson Medical College in Philadelphia.

In many ways, the profile of the mass killer looks a lot like the profile of the clinical narcissist, and that's a very bad thing. Never mind the disorder's name, narcissism is a condition defined mostly by debilitating low self-esteem, requiring the sufferer to seek almost constant recognition and reward. When the world and the people in it don't respond, as they should, narcissists are not just enraged but flat-out mystified.

Compulsion To Kill

The human brain is a complex organ, more sophisticated than the most powerful computer in existence. With it we think reason, love, hate, and problem solve. Some of us wrestle with the wonders of science and the workings of the universe, some simply on the best way to feed themselves and family in the coming days.

In the UK where I was a police officer for 21 years, we have a verdict on the statute books that deals with suicide. If the case evidence shows the victim died by his own hand and without outside assistance, the Coroner will record a verdict of "Suicide while the balance of the mind was disturbed." This verdict clearly shows that society accepts that a person of sound mind, would never contemplate suicide, but is that true? I recall a case when I was assigned jailer duty one morning. We had a prisoner in the cells who had been arrested the day before.

This man was a normal middle class family man, with a loving wife, two children, and a nice suburban home. He had a good job and was well liked in the community. So why was this man in the cell?

His downfall came when during a heated family argument, his daughter made an allegation of sexual abuse.

Compulsion To Kill

To this day it is unclear if this was a true allegation or one made by a young teenager trying to protect her mother. The result was, the man left his home and went to speak to a family friend. He told the friend that he valued his friendship more than anything and that in the coming days he may hear things that may alter his opinion about him. This worried the friend to the extent that he called the police.

The investigation had not even started, the man's wife and daughter were interviewed, and he was spoken to. I was not present during any of these interviews and therefore will not speculate as to what was said. I do know however that when I came on duty that morning, the night jailer briefed me that since his arrest the prisoner had not spoken to him at all but remained sitting on his bunk all night. He was still there when I went for my breakfast break around 8 a.m.

Before handing control to my relief, I asked the prisoner if he wanted anything to eat or drink, he replied "Just a coffee please." This may have been his last words. When I returned from my break there was pandemonium in the cellblock. The prisoner had killed himself despite the precautions taken such as removal of belt, tie, and any property he had. The cell had no beams and no obvious method to do harm.

Compulsion To Kill

However the cell did have a heating pipe that ran through the cell about 4 inches from the floor. He apparently did a handstand against the wall, tied a sheet or pillowcase around his neck securing it to the pipe, and did a back flip.

During the many years that have passed I have often thought of that man's last night. He was aware that in the coming days he faced a very public investigation, his wife and daughters would be interrogated and no doubt the story widely circulated at the kid's school and the community. His job and friends would likely disappear, and should the case come to court, further disclosures would become public records.

Either way, his life was over. He could however ensure that his wife, children and friends escaped the ordeal facing them. So! Suicide, while the balance of the mind was disturbed? Well, maybe or maybe his mind made the only decision it could. To take a well- known cable news stations catchphrase, "We report you decide."

In this book, I have not tried to justify or explain the motives behind the mass murderers. I will leave that to the psychiatrists and theorists. But I will try to dispel some of the misconceptions about these people.

I will look at a number of cases and show how the reporting of the incidents and attempts by

Compulsion To Kill

politicians to exploit them have clouded the issues.

Compulsion To Kill

Compulsion To Kill

Chapter 1

<u>THE BATH MASSACRE</u>

Ask most people in the USA to name the worst recorded school mass killing and you will probably get the names, Virginia Tech, or Columbine. Few if any, will say Bath, Michigan.

Why was this incident forgotten? Well! Maybe two reasons,

1 It occurred before the hi-tech age of computers, cable news, and IPod's.

2. The killer did not use a firearm.

I feel that this is significant; at the time in question the US was between wars. The news was dominated by the great Mississippi flood aftermath. There was a less than stable economy, and small town America was recovering from a disastrous world war.

The morning of May 18th 1927 started quietly enough for the people of the sleepy town of Bath, Michigan. Before the day ended the story of what happened that day spread around the world.

At the towns Consolidated school, lessons were well underway. Schoolteacher Leona Gudekust was teaching a class of first graders.

Compulsion To Kill

The children were listening to a story and begged the teacher for just one more story before starting the less appealing blackboard work.

The next day there was going to be a picnic and the children were relaxed and enjoying the school day, suddenly a massive explosion tore the school apart. Miss Gudekust later remarked that had she not told the extra story, the children would not have been at their desks but gathered around the blackboard in the corner of the room that was adjacent to the west wing which took the main force of the blast. As she said at the time, "that story saved many lives."

Both Miss Gudekust and Miss Bernice Sterling, the teacher in the next room, got their charges together in the confusion of the choking dust and led them to safety. Those on the top floor of the same wing, which had miraculously held up under the force of the explosion, escaped through windows and down the partly wrecked stairway. Some had however been injured.

Thirty-seven (37) children were dead, as well as one teacher, Hazel Weatherby, aged 22. Three of the outer walls of the building were blown away and the roof came down upon those who were on the second floor.

Compulsion To Kill

A few children against the inner wall escaped, but those on the outside were crushed under the beams and plaster. Part of the whole mass had slid down onto the children on the two lower floors.

The first people to arrive were greeted with a scene of absolute horror. The school was all but demolished the bodies of young children were crushed and twisted among the rubble.

While everyone rushed to assist, one man, a School board member, Andrew Kehoe, was seen smiling and waving at townspeople, seemingly oblivious to their frantic efforts to slow him down.

Kehoe had two dark secrets; firstly having just driven away from his burning farm, to where firefighters and rescuers were on scene, he knew that they may soon find the burned body of his wife Nellie, whom he had murdered the night before.

Secondly, Kehoe had packed the school with over 1000 pounds of explosive enough to destroy, not just the school but the entire town.

A large amount, 550 pounds had failed to detonate. Police on the scene searching the ruins found this, together with an alarm clock and wiring. They bravely defused it before carrying it from the building.

Compulsion To Kill

Kehoe must have realized this, and as he drove back to the school, he had a backup plan.

His car was packed with large amounts of tools, scrap metal, and explosives.

As he reached the scene, Kehoe saw the school superintendent Emory Huyck together with the towns Postmaster Glenn Smith and Smith's father in law. No doubt he was surprised to see them still alive.

He called them over. Kehoe had been at odds for several months with the superintendent over tax on school buildings.

As they reached the vehicle Kehoe announced that it was he who had set the explosion and yelled

"I'll take you with me," before producing a bolt action Winchester, .22 rifle and firing it into the stack of dynamite in the car. The massive explosion killed all 3, together with an 8 year old, Cleo Clapton, who had just wandered clear of the school in a dazed state and was hit by flying shrapnel.

Compulsion To Kill

So who was Andrew Kehoe?

Andrew Philip Kehoe was born in Tecumseh, Michigan in 1872. In 1912 he married and 7 years later he and his wife moved to Bath where they bought a small farm. He quickly built a reputation for thriftiness and in 1924 he was elected as treasurer to the consolidated school. In this position he frequently butted heads with the school superintendent over the tax rates levied by the board. This fight escalated with accusations of mismanagement being leveled at the superintendent.

In 1926 these festering grievances culminated in him hatching a deadly plan. It was in that year that Kehoe began buying and stockpiling dynamite, together with a popular explosive called Pyrotol, which was an inexpensive compound manufactured from military surplus cordite and smokeless powder. It was popular in the rural farming community for use in removing tree stumps.

By the following year, Nellie had developed tuberculosis and this also put a drain on the family finances. By this time Kehoe was showing more and more signs of a personality disorder. In modern times there would have been an array of help available from psychiatric professionals, who would recognize schizophrenia, but this was 1927, and the world was very different.

Compulsion To Kill

Records show that in 1911 at the age of 29, Kehoe suffered a severe head injury that left him drifting in and out of a coma for two months. While it is not known if this had any detrimental effect on his personality, compulsive behavior developed which had him changing clothes many times a day in order to always appear neat and clean. His farming neighbors questioned his agricultural skills.

As one of those neighbor's M.J. "Monty" Ellsworth put it thus,

"He never farmed it as other farmers do and he tried to do everything with his tractor. He was in the height of his glory when fixing machinery or tinkering. He was always trying new methods in his work, for instance, hitching two mowers behind his tractor. This method did not work at different times and he would just leave the hay standing. He also put four sections of drag and two rollers at once behind his tractor. He spent so much time tinkering that he didn't prosper."

Those that knew him well described him as a bit of an enigma, always willing to help others but prone to harsh angered criticism with anyone who did not share his views. He also became intolerant of criticism and taxes.

Compulsion To Kill

Kehoe was also known to exhibit sudden bouts of violence, once beating a horse to death on his farm.

It is true, that Kehoe, as an abused stepchild of fourteen had watched his stepmother burn to death from a malfunctioning stove. There were rumors that the burning may not have been an accident. These were largely fuelled by the revelation that the young man had not taken any action immediately to douse the flames. The facts however do not bear this out. Kehoe was only 14 at the time and while his Stepmother was attempting to light the stove it erupted in flame, dousing her with oil which then ignited. The young Kehoe threw a bucket of water over his stepmother but this caused a massive flame back.

Today most children are taught that you don't throw water on an oil fire such as a deep fry pan. In 1911 it is more than likely this was not common knowledge. Can we really blame the boy for throwing water over a fire? If the incident did affect him, it was more likely the shock of seeing his screaming stepmother burn alive before him, and the realization later that he may have hastened her death by his actions.

We will of course never know. Andrew was never detained, interviewed psychoanalyzed, or asked to account for his actions.

Compulsion To Kill

No court ordered a mental evaluation. Such procedures were unknown in 1927. Had he not killed himself and had been arrested he would have been tried, condemned and executed very swiftly, no doubt to the cheers of the American people.

At the time, the community, which was deeply religious, referred to him as the devils disciple, the monster from hell or the most evil human being on the planet. Many people would not disagree with that assessment. But one thing is clear. The bath school bombing was the worst mass school killing in recorded history. Kehoe's death by bomb suicide was the first ever recorded in the USA. He was the original suicide bomber.

Did he have a grudge against the children he killed?

I do not think so. He probably did not know most of them personally. His beef was with the school superintendent. It was with the tax system he was unable to change, and he wanted to hit back at the community. I believe his actions were thought out; his plan was to cause maximum distress and anguish. What better way than to destroy the possessions they cherished most. The same twisted motivation was apparent in the slaughter of children at Beslan in Russia and Dunblane in Scotland.

Compulsion To Kill

Andrew Kehoe's name may have faded from memory and been replaced by those of recent events in Aurora and Tucson, but remember Kehoe never shot anyone. He had access to firearms but chose another method to cause maximum death and misery on the community that he blamed for his misfortunes.

Bath Consolidated School was never rebuilt. The site today is a park with a simple bronze plaque marking the place where so many died on that fateful day in 1927.

Compulsion To Kill

Chapter 2

<u>THE PSEUDOCOMMANDO</u>

The term pseudocommando was first used by Professor Park Elliott Dietz a forensic psychiatrist and criminologist in 1986 to describe a type of mass murderer who plans his actions "after long deliberation." Professor Dietz is best known for his forensic consulting in many of the most controversial criminal and civil cases of the past 35 years. Some of these on behalf of state and federal prosecutors, needing an expert witness to testify in the more complex cases.

Among the good Professor's most notable criminal cases are those of John Hinkley Jr., the shooter of President Reagan and serial killer Jeffrey Dahmer who killed 17 people. There is also Andrea Yates who killed her own 5 children while depressed, Deanna Laney and Susan Smith also killed their children, and the infamous DC snipers, John Allan Mohammad and Lee Boyd Malvo who shot 10 people dead and severely wounded 3 others in the Beltway area of Washington DC in October 2003.

Compulsion To Kill

Dr Diez's view is that the pseudo commando often kills indiscriminately in public, in broad daylight, but may also kill family members and a "pseudo-community" that he believes has mistreated him.

He comes prepared with a powerful arsenal of weapons and has no escape planned. In effect he does not expect to survive the incident. He appears to be driven by strong feelings of anger and resentment, in addition to having a paranoid character. Such persons are "collectors of injustice" who nurture their wounded narcissism and retreat into a fantasy life of violence and revenge.

Professor Paul Mullen is another eminent psychiatrist who has written extensively on the subject of the pseudocommando.

Professor Mullen described the results of his detailed personal evaluations of five pseudocommando mass murderers who were caught before they could kill themselves or be killed. He noted that the massacres were often well planned (i.e., the offender did not "snap"), with the offenders arriving at the crime scene heavily armed, often in camouflage or warrior gear, and that they appeared to be pursuing a highly personal agenda of payback to an uncaring, rejecting world.

Compulsion To Kill

Both Mullen and Dietz have described this type of offender as a suspicious grudge holder who is preoccupied with firearms.

Mass killings by such individuals are not new, nor did they begin in the 1960s with the Texas Sniper. The news media tend to suggest that the era of mass public killings was ushered in by Whitman atop the tower at the University of Texas at Austin and have become "a part of American life in recent decades." Research indicates that the news media have heavily influenced the public perception of mass murder, particularly the erroneous assertion that its incidence is increasing. Furthermore, it is typically the high-profile cases that represent the most widely publicized, yet least representative mass killings. As an example that such mass murderers have existed long before Whitman, consider a notorious case, the Bath School massacre of 1927, which is covered elsewhere in this book.

Another person who contributes much to the debate is a former New Zealand Police Sergeant, William O'Brien. He was one of the officers responsible for handling the intense media interest in the Aramoana massacre in 1990, when 33 year-old Davis Malcolm Gray, an unemployed resident of Aramoana, shot dead - 14 people and wounded 4 others, before being shot multiple times by police.

Compulsion To Kill

O'Brien expands on Professor Dietz's description and adds further insight into the make up of these people.

Writing in 2009 he said this;

"Multiple murderers are divided into two main categories, 'Mass' and 'Serial'. Dietz defined mass murderers as psychotic killers, set and run killers (e.g. setting a bomb in a building), family annihilators or pseudo commandos. This final group are generally young male loners who have a preoccupation with firearms. Their prominent psychopathology is paranoia. Apart from paranoid beliefs they will hold long-term deep-seated grudges. They often live out their fantasies and are invariably powerless, insignificant people. One strong trait is their ability to plan their rampages, often in meticulous detail, and usually unleash it with a chilling calmness. In almost every case the perpetrators have a detailed awareness of other mass killings and often copy them.

There are thirty-four distinct traits that pseudo commandos share and these, I believe, are the key to minimising events. From the extensive research I carried out on mass killings around the world I believe that all mass killers come from a pool of people who share the thirty-four traits. However, this is not to suggest that everyone within that pool is a potential mass killer – far from it. But every

Compulsion To Kill

mass killer will come from that pool and it isn't rocket science to suggest that when someone applies for a firearms license – if they come from that pool – authorities should vet them more closely.

In many countries people can easily access a firearms license if they are non-violent, don't abuse drugs or alcohol, or have no criminal record. But invariably pseudo commandos are not outwardly violent, they seldom come to police attention and most don't drink alcohol, certainly not to excess. It is my belief that the more important aspects authorities should look at when determining whether someone is a fit and proper person to own firearms are things like paranoid beliefs, the holding of grudges, dysfunctional upbringing, a tendency to become territorial, or powerless and rather insignificant loners. Rigid vetting of people showing these traits is as important as any other considerations. Above all, people who display an emotional attachment to firearms should be examined closely. A more stringent background check is one of the key ingredients to keeping firearms out of reach of potential mass killers.

Another lesson we might learn is from the Columbine tragedy. In this case the perpetrators had long believed they were alienated and ridiculed by fellow pupils and subsequently took

Compulsion To Kill

their revenge. All too often people who tend towards mass killing identify the school and their peers as justification for their actions. I realize it can be difficult at times to accept people into a group when they exhibit strange behavior, but the individual's demeanor often exacerbates the problem. The more we shun them the more dangerous they become. They are a bit like a time bomb and we unwittingly light the fuse.

We may never prevent all mass killings involving high schools but it is a global phenomenon we can surely minimise. All we need is tolerance towards those who exhibit differences, but more importantly a determination to prevent those with a propensity towards pseudo commando personality from getting access to firearms. It won't prevent all occurrences, but it is a start. "

Any reader familiar with my first book, Debarred the use of Arms (Outskirts Press) will be aware that I am a strong supporter of the Second Amendment and I feel he has made a good general point. Keeping guns out of the hands of the mentally ill is very important, how you do that in a society that has a general right to both privacy and firearms ownership is more tricky.

Compulsion To Kill

Although it should also be remembered that O'Brien was writing with regards to UK gun laws and restrictions imposed in the UK and New Zealand before both countries imposed a general handgun ban.

So! Does it follow that the psuedocommando has to use a firearm to be worthy of that moniker?

In fact Guns aren't the most lethal mass murder weapon. According to data compiled by Grant Duwe of the Minnesota Department of Corrections, guns killed an average of 4.92 victims per mass murder in the United States during the 20th century, just edging out knives, blunt objects, and bare hands, which killed 4.52 people per incident. Fire killed 6.82 people per mass murder, while explosives far outpaced the other options at 20.82. Of the 25 deadliest mass murders in the 20th century, only 52 percent involved guns. As we saw in the Bath incident in the previous chapter, a mass murderer does not have to use a firearm to commit wholesale slaughter. While it is true that firearms make his job easier, it is not the prime motivation for his crime.

Revolutionary War veteran Barnett Davenport is widely considered the first mass murderer in U.S. history.

Compulsion To Kill

On the evening of Feb. 3, 1780, Davenport burst into the bedroom of his employer, Caleb Mallory, and began to bludgeon Mallory and his wife with a club. When the club broke in two, Davenport beat the couple to death with Mallory's gun. After beating the Mallory's to death, Davenport burned the house down, killing their three grandchildren. As most criminologists define mass murder as the killing of at least three people in a single incident, Davenport has the dubious honor of being this countries first recorded mass murderer.

Other mass murderers have also perpetrated their crimes without firearms.

For example Frenchman Pierre Riviere killed his mother, sister, and brother with a billhook in 1835. (A billhook is a cutting tool used in agriculture and forestry.) In 1932, Julian Marcelino, a Filipino immigrant of relatively small stature, managed to kill six and wound 15 on a Seattle street using only a bolo knife.

Mass murder is not a recent development however.

Buried deep in Scottish folk law is the infamous story of Sawney Beane. This was a story I first read about in the 60s in the United Kingdom.

Sawney Beane, described as idle and vicious took up with a woman of equally reputable nature.

Compulsion To Kill

They relocated to a cave that was difficult to detect on the wild coastline of Ayrshire, Scotland. Led by Beane, the family or Clan began murdering and robbing travelers. In order to satisfy their need for food they began cannibalizing everyone they killed.

This arrangement lasted several years during which time they sired 6 sons, 6 daughters and 18 grandsons most the offspring were of incest.

Frequently the family would dispose of legs and arms by throwing them into the sea, and which were then discovered by townspeople. As the number of those 'disappearing' grew, the locals became frantic, and searched almost the entire district attempting to find who or what could be responsible. It was during this period that some innocents were lynched and put to death. The cave had been noted by the searchers but it was believed no one could actually live inside as the tide filled it at its height. What they did not realize was that the cave had higher levels which remained dry even at high tide.

On one particular evening a married couple left the nearby village of Girvan, only to be set about by the roving band of Beane's clan. Unfortunately for the attackers the man was a skilled swordsman and pistol shooter and held them off.

Compulsion To Kill

Not long enough to save his wife however, who was dragged to her gory death, but long enough for him to escape and tell the district authorities of what he had encountered. This gave the searchers a point of reference.

Search parties were again sent out and eventually, soldiers finally found the cave but were not prepared for what they found inside. Boxes of jewels and other valuables, arms, legs, and thighs of men, women, and children hung in rows while other body parts were soaking in pickling.

The whole family was arrested and executed without trial, the men suffering death by extreme mutilation known at the time as being hung, drawn, and quartered. The women burned at the stake. If true this would certainly count as a horrific tale of evil and mass murder, (which may be the point of the stories of longevity), but there is evidence to suggest that this in no mere sandman tale to scare children.

The best source for the story is "The Newgate" calendar. This was originally a monthly bulletin of executions taking place within Newgate prison in London, England. The Calendar became more a chronicle of crime and appealed to a vast number of people and gained wide circulation, a sort of 14th century version of True Crimes Magazine.

Compulsion To Kill

Within one edition was the story of Sawney Beane. It recorded him as being born under the reign of James I of Scotland in East Lothian near Edinburgh.

The entry refers to Beane as the leader and elder of the family who lived in a cave on the coast of the shores of Ayr and Galloway, a murderous, cannibalistic family that killed and devoured over 1,000 people.

The Newgate calendar is widely accepted as an accurate record of early crime in the United Kingdom and, although the details may have been exaggerated for readership consumption, (Think of the National Enquirer), the story is therefore most likely essentially correct.

Perhaps Bob Geldof gave a partial answer when, following a school shooting in 1979 he wrote the song, "I don't like Mondays." Later taken to Number one in the UK charts, the title came from the answer given by the perpetrator 16 year old Brenda. The first verse as follows may be what the public perception is of these pseudo-commandos. But is it really that simple?

"The silicon chip inside her head
Gets switched to overload.
And nobody's gonna go to school today,
She's going to make them stay at home.
And daddy doesn't understand it,

Compulsion To Kill

He always said she was as good as gold.
And he can see no reason

'Cause there are no reasons
What reason do you need to be shown?"

The pseudocommando is a type of mass murderer who kills in public during the daytime, plans his offense well in advance, and comes prepared with a powerful arsenal of weapons. He has no escape planned and expects to be killed during the incident. Research suggests that the pseudo-commando is driven by strong feelings of anger and resentment, flowing from beliefs about being persecuted or grossly mistreated.

He views himself as carrying out a highly personal agenda of payback.

Some mass murderers take special steps to send a final communication to the public or news media; these communications, to date, have received little detailed analysis.

Study of an offender's use of language may reveal important data about his state of mind, his motivation, and psychopathology. The research on the pseudo-commando, as well as the psychology of revenge, with special attention to revenge fantasies, will reveal a wealth of information.

Compulsion To Kill

It is argued that revenge fantasies become the last refuge for the pseudo commando's mortally wounded self-esteem and therefore ultimately enable him to commit mass murder-suicide.

Compulsion To Kill

Compulsion To Kill

Chapter 3

<u>INSIDE THE MIND OF THE KILLERS</u>

In trying to determine the mindset of the mass killer, I have tried to find a common link between the mass shooters, such as those at Columbine, Virginia Tec, and Tucson. Not to mention Aurora.

My research led me to the work of various eminent psychologists, some of whom worked on the cases concerned.

Following the Columbine killings in 1999, the US Government tried the same thing, and they commissioned a study of 37 incidents of school violence that occurred between the years 1974 to 2000.

Overall the investigators found that more than half of all the attackers had documented cases of extreme depression. Twenty five percent (25%) had serious problems with drugs and alcohol. Most witnesses gave statements such as, he was such a quiet boy, and, he did not mix much.

Compulsion To Kill

Only when you interview family and friends do you find the subject had a history of hospitalizations, or showed anger and resentment over some incident in their lives for weeks afterwards.

Only 24 hours after the Virginia Tech massacre in 2007, (when South Korean student Seung Hui Cho killed 30 students and wounded 17 more.) chilling writings and play-lets he had written began appearing on websites detailing abuse of young boys among other fantasies. Cho had shot himself after the killings and before he could be detained and questioned. Therefore we were never able to seriously examine his mindset. However scrutinizing these writings does give us an insight to the workings of his mind, but here again we must be careful.

Professor N. G. Berrill, a forensic psychologist at John Jay College of Criminal Justice in New York City, is a leading researcher in this field; the Professor puts it this way;

"These things can percolate for years, quite often there is an early event where they are submitted to violence or are marginalized."

So just what role may marginalization play in that person's mindset?

Compulsion To Kill

Well! How we look at what we mean by the term, marginalization could also be described as, being left out, not being a team player or mixer.

This often leads to a profound sense of powerlessness, the sense that everyone is against you or out to get you. I recall seeing a recent TV ad depicting the disgruntled consumer, who feels powerless and needs to take the power back, He does this by taking karate lessons and becoming the Fist of goodness, and of course fails. I am sure the reader knows the advertisement I refer to.

Yes it's amusing but like a lot of TV advertising today, it also carries a subliminal message.

Marginalized people tend to hit back. More worryingly, it doesn't take grave abuses like molestation to leave people feeling so minimized. Perceived indifference from a parent or spouse, or dismissal from a job, even if unfounded can have a similar effect.

When the world outside the home seems to be conspiring in the mistreatment of an individual, that sense of invalidation grows worse in that individual.

Compulsion To Kill

These setbacks are part of life; most of us deal with them and move on. But to someone already highly sensitized to such setbacks, they can be an intolerable strain.

So are there any clues that may sound an early warning?

Well! Close study of most mass shootings in this country indicate that the perpetrators do suffer from a mental condition called Schizophrenia. This is a condition that leaves the patient unable to separate what is and what is not real. The patient finds it hard to think clearly, act normally in social situations or to have normal emotional responses.

Psychiatrists are not sure what causes the condition and there is no doubt that Schizophrenia is a very complex condition. However, what is known is that you are more likely to develop the condition if there is a history of it in your family. Schizophrenia is not confined to a particular class or group. It can affect anyone at any time. Mental health experts are divided, as to what causes it. However, it is strongly suggested that genes may play a role.

The condition usually begins in the early teenage years. If the gene theory is correct it is possible that the condition needs a trigger of some kind to activate it.

Compulsion To Kill

Schizophrenia affects both men and women equally. However, it tends develop later in women, who do not get it as severe.

So let us take a closer look at some of the more notorious mass killers who have been diagnosed with this condition.

JARED LEE LOUGHNER

January 8th 2011, in a parking lot, in Tucson, Arizona, another shooting took place that shocked the world and led to another hysterical clamor for gun control. On that day Popular Democrat Congresswoman Gabrielle Giffords was holding a regular '*Meet the Electorate*' event at the parking lot of a Safeway supermarket. Security was minimal and Ms. Giffords was shaking hands and speaking to the voters who were queuing in an orderly fashion for the opportunity to meet her.

The congresswoman's aides were not expecting trouble and were mainly occupied with crowd control, and ensuring that each member of the public got equal time to discuss their concerns. Nearby, the Safeway store was busy, it was a Saturday, and the supermarket was doing good business.

No one really noticed the medium built bald headed young man standing in the queue with a jacket pulled tightly over his chest.

Compulsion To Kill

In other times the public may have taken him for a Shaolin monk or an eccentric peace-worshipping hippy. In fact, they could not have been more wrong.

Jared Lee Loughner was not a fan of the Congresswoman, or of the Democratic Party. In fact he had a deep-rooted hatred of all things Governmental, regardless of party affiliation. Beneath his coat he was gripping a Glock, 9mm semi-automatic pistol fitted with a 40 round capacity extended magazine.

As he stepped forward to apparently shake Ms. Giffords hand he suddenly produced the pistol and fired point blank at the startled woman's head. As the congresswoman fell, he continued to shoot indiscriminately at the panicking crowd around him. His shots found Federal Judge John Roll who had been speaking to the congresswoman immediately before. Loughner continued rapid fire seemingly picking targets at random. Men, women and children, it appeared to make no difference, (a trait also seen a year later in Aurora, Colorado when James Holmes opened fire in a crowded cinema.)

As Ms. Giffords fell to the floor, Loughner's gun jammed. (A common fault with high capacity magazines).

Compulsion To Kill

Seizing the opportunity, a brave member of the crowd hit him with a folding chair and others then rushed to overpower him.

Among these was an armed concealed carry holder Joe Zamudio, who was emerging from the Safeway store when he heard the shooting.

Although initially reaching for his own gun, he saw a woman wrestle the gun from Loughner's hand and eject the magazine. Assessing the situation clearly, he left his weapon holstered and assisted in detaining Loughner until police arrived.

Incredibly, Gabby Giffords survived the head wound, but other victims were not so lucky. Victims included Federal Judge John Roll and 13-year-old Christine Taylor Green.

As so often happens, the media went into frenzy. CNN reporting falsely that Giffords had been shot dead, others - that gun crime could only be stopped by immediately banning guns.

The status of his victim and the fact that she was a Democrat Congresswoman led to a frenzy of ludicrous media speculation. Blame was leveled at Former vice Presidential candidate Sarah Palin, a republican for an earlier campaign ad in which she targeted several seats held by Democrats, by placing cross hairs over each one. A tactic not unknown in politics and actually first used by the Democratic Party.

Compulsion To Kill

Also blamed was the NRA, for its stance on defending the 2nd Amendment, the size of the magazine used, and incredibly, the Tea Party group who were opposed to the agenda of President Obama.

All this, together with the overwhelming support for Ms Giffords as she recovered, brought out the best as well as the worst in the American people. President Barak Obama gave a powerful speech at a memorial service after the shooting, in which he called for an end to the vitriol and name-calling. The speech was well received by all sides in the political arena and Ms. Giffords husband, NASA astronaut Mark Kelly. Mr. Kelly put his duties on hold as commander of the next shuttle mission to be with his wife. Such human-interest stories did much to calm down the anger and the issue of gun control, and gun control was taken off the agenda. Despite surviving, Ms Giffords injuries were so severe that she was forced to give up her congressional seat.

More levelheaded politicians sought to find a common thread, suggesting that the laws should be tightened to stop mentally ill people buying guns. They had no answer when asked the inevitable follow up question, how do we identify these mentally ill people?

Compulsion To Kill

It reminds me of the preacher who was asked what his view was on sin in the world, after a moment's thought he leaned forward to the interviewer, and said, "I'm against it."

Loughner's world was indeed a strange and unsettling place. In the days that followed, reporters tracked down witnesses and locals who knew the suspect.

"He was very disconnected from reality and from our class," says Lydian Ali, a classmate of his in a poetry writing class at Pima Community College. "I remember him being incoherent when he contributed to class discussions. He would make a comment about someone's poem and none of us would know what he was talking about." Another student, Amy Jensen, wrote on her website, that she dropped out of a class at Pima, in part because of Loughner's bizarre behavior.

"He was creepy. He would laugh to himself nearly all the time, even about things that weren't funny," Jensen wrote. "I sat behind him in that class and dropped it partially because of him. He was the kind of guy I pictured bringing a gun to class and shooting everyone."

Compulsion To Kill

Such behavior was not lost on Pima Community College officials, who suspended Loughner in September 2010 after administrators grew disturbed over one of his internet posts, and told his parents he would not be re-admitted without a mental health clearance. Loughner dropped out the following month. Once out of school he dropped off the radar. It was Out of sight, out of mind, as far as the authorities were concerned.

Mark Potok is a spokesman and director of publications and information for the Southern Poverty Law Centre in Montgomery, Alabama, a nonprofit organization that arose from the anti-segregation movement to counter extremism and hate crimes. He was asked to examine the mindset of Loughner.

In examining Loughner's list of favorite books, which includes George Orwell's "*1984*" and Adolf Hitler's, "*Mein Kampf,*" Potok notes that an anti-government thread runs through all those works. In addition, Loughner's obsession with currency not being backed by gold and silver "is a core idea of the militia, or Patriot, movement." Further examination of his notes and writings reveal a dark turbulent mind. At one point in his notes Loughner writes, "My favorite activity is conscience dreaming." According to Potok's thinking, this might refer to "conscious dreaming," an idea particularly perpetrated by the eccentric British writer David Icke.

Compulsion To Kill

"The link to Icke, who is an extremist, might be weak, but the basic idea of conscious dreaming is probably impossible for the average layman to understand. In essence it boils down to this; what we think is reality really isn't. We live in a 'holographic universe," and are duped into believing what we see, without questioning it.

Potok goes on to say, " *If that is a philosophy Loughner had adopted, that might in some ways explain other books on his favorite book list like, "Alice in Wonderland" and other alternate reality books.* "

Potok's conclusion is that "Most likely he is a mentally ill man who heard a lot of vitriolic rhetoric and started to absorb some of it," Another noted British criminal psychologist, Dr. Vaughn Bell has also examined the case of Jared Loughner, in particular the idea that he suffered from a form of Schizophrenia. He contends that this is, quite simply wrong. It is wrong scientifically, where excellent research shows that the link between mental illness and violence is minimal, and it is wrong socially, where it is easier to name or label a person as mentally ill, then close off any deeper explanation of what happened and why. Citing the work of another Oxford psychiatrist is Dr. Seena Fazel, who has done epidemiological work on mental illness and violence.

Compulsion To Kill

Dr. Fazel carried out extensive research examining data on 18,000 individuals with schizophrenia and other psychoses. Her view is that Schizophrenia and other psychoses are associated with violence and violent offending, particularly homicide. However, most of the excess risk appears to be mediated by substance abuse comorbidity. The risk in these patients with comorbidity is similar to that for substance abuse without psychosis. Public health strategies for violence reduction could consider focusing on the primary and secondary prevention of substance abuse. Or to put it more simply, if you're looking for violence, head to your local bar.

Dr Bell offers the following analogy.

"If Loughner were obsessed with soccer, would normal people take that as an explanation for his violent acts? No. Knowing somebody is a soccer fan does not tell you much about his or her propensity for violence. The same is true of mental illness – knowing someone is mentally ill tells us little about that person's propensity for violence."

If you, as a clinical psychologist, were examining this case and found evidence on the Web that Jared Lee Loughner or some other suspected killer was obsessed with soccer or football or hockey and suggested it might be an explanation for his crime, you'd be laughed at.

Compulsion To Kill

But do the same with "schizophrenia" and people nod in solemn agreement. Clearly the label of mentally ill is on many occasions, a cop out, (to use an American term.)

The fact is that mental illness is so often used to explain violent acts, despite the evidence to the contrary, almost certainly flows from how such cases are handled in the media.

Numerous studies show that crimes by people with psychiatric problems are over-reported, and are more often than not filled with gross inaccuracies that give a totally false impression of risk. With this constant misrepresentation, it's not surprising that the public sees mental illness as an easy explanation for heartbreaking events such as the Tucson incident

To add a little clarity to this, consider the following.

Your chance of being murdered by a stranger with schizophrenia is so vanishingly small that a recent study of four Western countries put the figure at one in 14.3 million. To put this into perspective, statistics show you are about three times more likely to be killed by a lightning strike.

Compulsion To Kill

Was it that toxic cocktail—mental illness, mixed with angry political rhetoric—that could have pushed the Tucson gunman over the edge into violent madness?

Well! In August 2012, Loughner finally faced a court after being deemed competent to stand trial. In a plea bargaining deal worked out by his defense team he pleaded guilty to all charges and was sentenced to life imprisonment without parole. In exchange the State did not pursue the death penalty. The guilty plea also meant that the witnesses would not be required to re-live the horror of that day in January when so many innocent lives were lost.

Maybe it is helpful to cross over here from the depths of insanity to the law, regarding the dealing of such a case. Not Guilty by reason of insanity is usually the verdict any trial defense lawyer would go for, if faced with the task of defending a man like Loughner, whose crime was witnessed by so many people and who was detained at the scene.

Professor Mark Heyrman, a lecturer at the University of Chicago's Law school, has considered this question and comes to this conclusion.

Compulsion To Kill

"After the Hinckley assassination attempt on Reagan and his successful insanity defense, Congress amended the federal insanity defense—returning it to Mc'Naghten—unable to appreciate the criminality of one's conduct. The defendant must prove this by clear and convincing evidence.

Of course it is stupid to diagnose someone based upon newspaper accounts and particularly stupid if you are a lawyer and not a mental health professional. However, I am willing to bet that Loughner has a serious AXIS I diagnosis—some type of psychotic disorder. My guess would be schizophrenia. I think that it is very sad that he did not get appropriate attention from someone who could help. Even if true, that does not mean he has an insanity defense. 15% of the folks in our prisons have serious mental illnesses. That fact does not mean that they should have been acquitted by reason of insanity."

So what does the case of Jared Loughner tell us?

Well! It shows us, if nothing else, that there is little that can be done to prevent a mass shooting if the killer is capable of rational thought.

It also tells us that blaming guns and political rhetoric will lead us up a blind alley.

Compulsion To Kill

Loughner was not made a killer by the Glock gun he possessed, any more than being at the controls of a jetliner turned Al Queda terrorist Mohammad Atta into a homicidal maniac.

Both used the tools at hand to fulfill their intents.

Later in the book we will explore outside influences such as the media, films and computer gaming, but for now we can be thankful that these events are rare and the intricate workings of the human mind are slowly being unraveled, by modern psychology. Whether this will ever eliminate the threat altogether, remains to be seen, but the chances are not good. Can we then at least prepare ourselves and be ready?

Well that depends on political will and obtaining a consensus on such controversial subjects as gun control, and wise laws being passed after much research. The likelihood of such agreement is almost as difficult to envisage as identifying a potential mental problem in a future killer.

Seung-Hui Cho

The horrific events of Virginia Tech on April 16th 2007 are unlikely to be forgotten, either by the students who were there, or the Police who were called to the campus.

Compulsion To Kill

Seung-Hui Cho, a student opened fires at the school killing 32 people and wounding 23 others. So! Who was this disturbed killer and can we learn anything about him that may spread light on his actions.

Seung-Hui Cho was born in South Korea. He arrived in the United States at the age of 8 with his family, where he later obtained permanent resident status. At middle school, he was diagnosed with a severe anxiety disorder, Selective Mutism, as well as a more serious depressive disorder. After this diagnosis Cho began receiving treatment and therapy and special education support until his junior year of high school.

During Cho's last two years at Virginia Tech, several instances of his abnormal behavior, as well as plays and other writings he submitted began to cause concern among both his teachers and fellow classmates. The writings contained frequent accounts of violence and bloodlust that should have raised real red flags. Well it did, and on December 13th 2005, Cho was found "mentally ill and in need of hospitalization" by New River Valley Community Services Board. The physician who examined Cho noted that he had a "flat effect and a depressed mood", even though Cho "denied suicidal thoughts and did not acknowledge symptoms of a thought disorder."

Compulsion To Kill

Based on this mental health examination and because Cho was suspected of being "an imminent danger to himself or others," he was detained temporarily at Carilion St. Albans Behavioral Health Center in Radford Virginia, pending a commitment hearing before the Montgomery County District Court.

It was recognized that Cho presented an imminent danger to himself as a result of his mental illness and Virginia Justice Judge Paul Barnett said so in a report to the court. Incredibly though, Barnett recommended he be treated as an outpatient and not detained as an involuntary patient. This decision was to have profound consequences.

Therefore on December 14, 2005, Cho was released from the mental health facility after Judge Barnett ordered Cho to undergo mental health treatment on an outpatient basis, with a directive for him to "follow all recommended treatments." Since Cho underwent only a minimal psychiatric assessment the true diagnosis for Cho's mental health status remains unknown and probably the last opportunity to prevent the coming horror had disappeared. Normally Cho's mental state would have prevented him from being able to purchase firearms. However, under Virginia State law, critical wording on the forms required to be sent to the State Police. These forms are restricted to the State Criteria relating to mental illness for use in background checks.

Compulsion To Kill

These state that only a person involuntarily committed or ruled Mentally Incapacitated were prohibited from buying firearms.

Cho was neither, as he was not committed as an inpatient, and had not been adjudged mentally incapacitated. The law allowed him to start arming himself.

On February 9, 2007, Cho purchased his first handgun, a. 22 Walther P22 semi-automatic pistol, from a federally licensed firearms dealer based in Green Bay, Wisconsin. The seller shipped the gun to a pawnbroker in Blacksburg, Virginia, where Cho completed the legally required background check for the purchase transaction and took possession of the handgun. Cho bought a second handgun, a 9mm Glock 19 semi-automatic pistol, on March 13, 2007 from another licensed gun dealer located in Roanoke, Virginia.

Cho was of course able to pass both background checks and successfully complete both handgun purchases. He presented his U.S. permanent residency card his Virginia driver's permit - to prove legal age and length of Virginia residence and a checkbook showing his Virginia address, to the gun dealer.

Compulsion To Kill

All this in addition to waiting the required 30-day period between each gun purchase, he was successful at completing both handgun purchases, even though he had failed to disclose information on the background questionnaire about his mental health that required court-ordered outpatient treatment at a mental health facility.

On March 22, 2007, Cho purchased two 10-round magazines for the Walther P22 pistol. Cho also bought a number of jacketed hollow point ammunition,

These rounds are primarily used for Law enforcement and home defense because they result in more tissue damage than full metal jacket rounds. This is because of the rapid expansion of the bullet when entering soft tissue. This is an asset when hunting but devastating when your target is human.

Having armed himself, Cho then started preparing for his revenge. First he filed off the serial number of both weapons to thwart identification. Then he began to attend a gun range at Roanoke approximately 40 miles from the Campus. Finally he prepared a package for mailing to NBC news. The package contained Photographs DVDs and other material.

Compulsion To Kill

The reason was not known, but it appeared to be an attempt to ensure both notoriety and accuracy in his identity. At around 0715 hours (7:15 am) on the morning of April 16th 2007 Cho entered the West Ambler Johnston Hall on the Virginia Tech Campus. He went to the fourth floor where he shot and killed two students Emily Hilscher and Ryan Clark. The motive for these killings was never determined.

After the shooting, Cho left the Campus and mailed the package to NBC a portion of one of the videos sent is transcribed below.

"You have vandalized my heart, raped my soul, and torched my conscience. You thought it was one pathetic boy's life you were extinguishing. Thanks to you, I die like Jesus Christ, to inspire generations of the weak and defenseless people. Do you know what it feels to be spit on your face and to have trash shoved down your throat? Do you know what it feels like to dig your own grave? Do you know what it feels like to have your throat slashed from ear to ear? Do you know what it feels like to be torched alive? Do you know what it feels like to be humiliated and be impaled upon on a cross? And left to bleed to death for your amusement? You have never felt a single ounce of pain your whole life. Did you want to inject as much misery in our lives as you can just because you can?...I didn't have to do this. I could have left.

Compulsion To Kill

I could have fled. But no, I will no longer run. It's not for me. For my children, for my brothers and sisters that you fucked;, I did it for them... When the time came, I did it. I had to...You had a hundred billion chances and ways to have avoided today, but you decided to spill my blood. You forced me into a corner and gave me only one option. The decision was yours. Now you have blood on your hands that will never wash off. You had everything you wanted. Your Mercedes wasn't enough, you brats. Your golden necklaces weren't enough, you snobs. Your trust fund wasn't enough. Your Vodka and Cognac weren't enough. All your debaucheries weren't enough.

Those weren't enough to fulfill your hedonistic needs. You had everything"

After posting the package Cho returned to his room, retrieved the 9mm pistol and ammunition and walked slowly and deliberately towards Norris Hall and in the following 9 minutes shot 54 unarmed students killing 30 of them. Police rushed to the scene and as they reached Cho he put the Glock to his head and fired.

In the weeks that followed, Police, the Media and students tried to understand what had happened. Various theories were expounded.

Compulsion To Kill

In his writings, Cho mentioned the Columbine High School killers, Eric Harris and Dylan Klebold. Was this other mass killing the inspiration for Cho?

In 1999, one of the worst school massacres occurred at the Columbine High School in Littleton, Colorado. Two senior students, Eric Harris and Dylan Klebold, wearing trench coats and armed with a mixed variety of weapons, approached the school entrance of this designated gun-free-zone. The two were determined to kill as many people as possible, and had the firepower to do it. The weapons they had at their disposal were an Intratech TEC DC9 High point mod 995 carbine and 2 savage pump action shotguns together with a sawn off shotgun.

There was one slim chance to avoid the coming massacre. It came in the form of a school officer, Deputy Gardener, who was first on the scene and came under fire from Eric Harris who turned his semi auto rifle on the officer firing ten shots at him before the rifle jammed. The deputy returned fire with his service issue handgun, momentarily checking Harris's fire.

However, the student cleared the jam and continued firing at the deputy before re-entering the school to continue his murder spree.

Compulsion To Kill

Deputy Gardener, now low on ammo, took cover while calling for back- up, which arrived in the form of Deputies Scott Taborsky and Paul Smoker.

On reaching the scene, Deputy Smoker saw Deputy Gardener with his pistol drawn at his vehicle as one gunman appeared at a school window with a semi-automatic weapon and began shooting again. Smoker returned fire and the gunman disappeared. Inside the school, panic-stricken high school pupils tried to flee as the two teenagers walked down the hallway and into the library, laughing out loud and spraying bullets at pupils indiscriminately.

Sounds of gunfire, bullets hitting metal lockers and windows, and the screams of the wounded and dying were clearly audible to the helpless officers outside.

Students began to spill out of the school; some injured others in deep shock. When gunfire subsided, a police S.W.A.T. team stormed the building. They were greeted with a scene of absolute horror.

Bodies of students littered the hallway and library. In the library along with their victims, lay the bodies of the two gunmen. They had simply run out of people to kill, and had turned their weapons on themselves.

Compulsion To Kill

Twelve students and one teacher died that day and twenty-one others had suffered gunshot wounds. So what is known of the two teenagers who caused so much carnage?

Eric David Harris was born in Wichita, Kansas. His father Wayne Harris was a pilot in the US Air Force and as a consequence Eric frequently moved home due to Air Force deployments. This continued until 1993 when Wayne retired from the military and the family settled down Littleton, Colorado. The Harris family lived in rented accommodations for the first three years that they lived in the Littleton area.

It was during this time, Eric met Dylan Klebold, and the two became friends. In 1996, the Harris family purchased a house south of the Columbine High School.

Dylan Bennet Klebold was born in Lakewood, Colorado, to Thomas and Susan Klebold. His parents regularly attended a local Lutheran church with their children. At Columbine High, Harris and Klebold were active in school play productions, operated video productions, and became computer assistants maintaining the school's computer server.

Compulsion To Kill

According to accounts following the shooting, Harris and Klebold were very unpopular students and were frequently bullied by other students. Both were also said to have been members of a school group called the "Trench coat Mafia." However, this was probably hype following the shooting, as the two did not feature in the School yearbook photos depicting members of the group in 1998. Reportedly members of that group said they had no particular connection with the group. There is however a record of a "911" call made in on April 20th 1999 by Harris's father, in which he states that his son was a member.

In common with many perpetrators of this type of crime Harris and Klebold linked their personal computers on a network and both played many games over the Internet. Harris created a set of levels for the popular on line game Doom. These later became known as the Harris Levels.

Both boys used various aliases while engaged in these on line activities. Harris had various websites that hosted the *Doom* and Quake files, as well as team information for those he gamed with online. On these sites he openly espoused hatred for the people of their neighborhood and the world in general.

Compulsion To Kill

When the pair began experimenting with making, and setting off pipe bombs, they then posted results of the explosions on the websites. Even this failed to raise any alarm. It is an irony that such gifted youngsters who could have had a very bright career in the IT industry, instead allowed their obsession with violent video games and hatred against fellow students to engulf them. The stage was set for an unimaginable horror.

Thomas Hamilton and the Politics

of Gun Control

Whenever there is a mass school shooting, the shock and horror as the events unfold nearly always lead to renewed calls from gun control. Here in the USA these calls usually go no further than table thumping rhetoric from the left wing media groups and anti gun politicians. The reason? The 2nd Amendment of the United States Constitution prevents any legislator from imposing infringements on the right of citizens to own firearms. Gun control is a very contentious issue and most politicians would rather not risk alienating their voters by proposing it. In fact, an NRA endorsement is a much sought after commodity in US Politics.

Compulsion To Kill

However, School shootings are not confined to the US. Across the Atlantic in my home country the United Kingdom, the law on gun ownership is far stricter, and there is no Second Amendment to worry politicians.

The sleepy picturesque Scottish town of Dunblane is a small cathedral town and former borough north of the city of Sterling in the Sterling Council area of the country. The town is situated off the A9 Road, which leads north to Perth. Its main landmark is Dunblane Cathedral Stirlingshire.

The towns' primary school on Doune Road, a two-story building is situated in the heart of the residential area. In 1996, the school was the scene of the remains of the deadliest massacre of children ever in the United Kingdom, in which 17 people were killed. Dunblane's sleepy image was shattered forever on 13th March 1996, when a crazed gunman named Thomas Hamilton, walked into what we would call the 1st grade class, armed with 4 handguns and opened fire killing sixteen pre-school children and one teacher. For a fuller account of this incident see my previous book "Debarred the Use of Arms." (Outskirts Press).

The shock of the cold-blooded murder of young children would generate horror in any civilized society. And I cannot criticize the British people for looking for blame and answers.

Compulsion To Kill

The blame of course lay squarely with Thomas Hamilton. It was he who planned and carried out this atrocity. But Hamilton was dead, so Britain looked elsewhere for blame and focused on the weapon he used, and the law allowing UK citizens to own handguns.

The resulting ban on handgun ownership had far-reaching consequences in sport, and for the Olympics. It had of course no positive effect on violent crime which rose dramatically.

So politics aside, what drove Thomas Hamilton to commit his crime, and can anything be learned from this incident?

Thomas Watt Hamilton was born on May 10th 1952. He was a shopkeeper and the leader of 3 local scout troops. In this capacity, he applied for and was granted a firearm certificate by the local police, This certificate permitted Hamilton to acquire guns as detailed on the certificate, which contained the type and caliber of weapon, as well as the amount of ammunition he was allowed to buy at any one time and to possess.

When Hamilton was in his mid-20s, he obtained a firearms certificate and started collecting firearms. In 1977 alone, he bought and sold five guns. He continued to buy even more as the years progressed.

Compulsion To Kill

Moreover, to enhance his firing skills, he became a member of several area gun clubs where he would diligently practice.

Hamilton had become increasingly involved in the Boy Scout movement during the 1970s.
His work with the movement was recognized and in 1973 he was appointed an Assistant Scout Leader of a Stirling scout troop.

However, misgivings soon arose about his suitability for his chosen role, particularly his leadership abilities. In the winter of 1973 Hamilton organized a trip for a dozen young boys to the resort area of Avimore in the Highlands. When they arrived, their van broke down. With no lodging in sight, Hamilton and the boys were forced to spend the night huddled together in the vehicle with temperatures below freezing. Several weeks later Hamilton led another troop of scouts on a winter expedition, which was designed to test the youngster's survival abilities.

However, Hamilton's lack of leadership skills again became very obvious. Hamilton's self-designed tests went far beyond the standard scouting limits, to the point that he placed his young charges in real danger. Many of the young boys returned home wet and suffering from mild hypothermia.

Compulsion To Kill

The parents of the children were understandably outraged and this concern was matched by other scout leaders who were outraged by Hamilton's recklessness and allegations from a number of reports about bizarre behavior such as being indecently exposed in the company of young boys.

Faced with a storm of protests, the county and district commissioners were forced to act. They asked Hamilton to resign. It is important to note that no charges were ever filed against Hamilton.

Hamilton just would not accept he had done anything wrong. He became visibly angry that his leadership abilities were being questioned. In an attempt to defend himself, he wrote several letters of complaint to Scotland's Scout Association and Headquarters, even going so far as to demand an inquiry into the events.

However, it was obvious that Hamilton had jeopardized the boys' safety and he was eventually forced to tender his resignation.

Most of us know of people, who have over confidence in their own ability, such people rarely take constructive criticism, even from friends. Thomas Hamilton was such a man.

Compulsion To Kill

In 1972, Hamilton established a do-it yourself business Woodcraft, following his fall from grace as a scoutmaster. Had things gone well, the world would most likely never have heard of him. However they did not. His business started to collapse as product sales decreased. This he blamed on resentment by the towns people over the rumors about his scouting escapades. The clock was ticking.

Following the failure of his shop, Hamilton decided to set up a series of boys clubs in and around Stirling and Dunblane. The projects preoccupied him for the remainder of his life. Hamilton sent many letters to the Police and other officials regarding the clubs and tried to re-define himself as a community leader. However he was not well liked and the rumors of inappropriate behavior would not go away. Around this time he acquired the name Mr. Creepy among the youths who had known him. Among the boys who were suspicious and uneasy about him was Andrew Murry, who would later become famous as Britain's Number One tennis champion.

In a fight back, Hamilton wrote various letters to the local MP and even Queen Elizabeth, complaining about the persecution of him by the Police and local population.

Compulsion To Kill

When I was a UK Police Officer, such behavior would have raised severe red flags and would have led to a re-evaluation of his suitability to own handguns. This was in fact, acted upon by Detective Sergeant Paul Hughes, the former head of Central Scotland Polices child protection unit. He wrote a damning report in which he recommended that Hamilton's gun license be revoked because of his unsavory character and unstable personality.

However, no action was taken because there was no concrete evidence of any wrongdoing. Thus, Thomas Hamilton was free to continue running his boys clubs. So! Was there any evidence of Hamilton being a sexual predator?

According to the report by Lord Cullen into the affair, published in 1996, there was only evidence of two incidents which suggested Hamilton was possibly a pedophile. The first was a statement from a 12-year-old, who testified that Hamilton sat down close to him and rubbed him on the inside of his leg. Yet, the incident was brushed aside and no report was ever filed.

The second was from another 12-year-old boy who testified anonymously that he was sexually abused. The boy claimed that Hamilton inappropriately touched his private parts and anally assaulted him with his fingers.

Compulsion To Kill

Certainly a serious allegation if true, however, Cullen expressed difficulty accepting the testimony because he did not have an opportunity to cross-examine the boy, and noted that he had in the past been convicted of a serious crime of dishonesty.

So we are left with a strong suspicion of ulterior motives but little if any proof. If innocent, Hamilton would understandably have been bitter and resentful. But could this excuse his actions?

James Eagan Holmes

The Century 16 cinema complex at Aurora, Colorado was packed on the evening Friday July 20TH 2012 for the premiere of the new Batman movie.

Outside in the parking lot a figure crossed to a wedged open fire exit. He was dressed in black and wore a military gas mask, a load bearing vest, a Military ballistic helmet, bullet resistant leggings, a throat protector, a groin protector, and tactical gloves. He was carrying Remington 870 tactical shotgun, a Smith and Wesson M&P 15 semi - automatic rifle fitted with a 100 round drum magazine.

Compulsion To Kill

Under any other circumstances this would have raised considerable alarm, but few in the audience considered the masked figure a threat. He appeared to be wearing a costume, like many other audience members who had dressed up for the screening. Others believed this was some sort of publicity stunt, or thought that he was part of a special effects installation set up for the film's premiere by the studio, or theater management.

The action had reached full volume on the screen when this illusion was shattered. The gunman suddenly threw a canister emitting a gas or smoke, which all but obscured the audience members' vision, made their throats and skin itch, and caused eye irritation. Coughing and screams filled the theatre as he then fired the shotgun, first at the ceiling and then at the audience. Dropping the shotgun, the gunman then opened fire with the M&P which fortunately malfunctioned after reportedly firing fewer than 30 rounds, a common fault with the drum type of accessory.

Finally, he fired a Glock 22 handgun. He shot first to the back of the room, and then toward people in the aisles. Some bullets passed through the wall and hit people in the adjacent theater #8, which was screening the same film. By this time the cinema was a bloodbath with the screams of the wounded and dying mixing with ringing of the cinemas auditorium smoke alarms.

Compulsion To Kill

After his murderous rampage, the killer walked out of into the parking lot and meekly surrendered to attending police officers, bizarrely announcing, *"I am the Joker, "* an apparent reference to one of Batman's literary enemies.

The gunman who allegedly killed 12 people during a screening of "The Dark Knight Rises" in Aurora, Colorado was James Eagan Holmes aged 24, A University of Colorado drop out who had been a PhD student in neuroscience.

He was due to be evicted from his apartment owned by the University, and was nearing the end of his grace period for staying at the institution's accommodation. Rules stated that anyone living in the block had to be enrolled at the university otherwise you had 30 days to evacuate.

A former classmate from the University of Colorado suggested another cause for the killings, describing Holmes as someone who had lost touch with reality after becoming 'obsessed' with video games.

The classmate told the Daily Mail: "James was obsessed with computer games and was always playing role-playing games."

Compulsion To Kill

"I can't remember which one but it was something like World of Warcraft, one of those where you compete against people on the internet."

"He did not have much of a life apart from that and doing his work. James seemed like he wanted to be in the game and be one of the characters."

"It seemed that being online was more important to him than real life. He must have lost his sense of reality, how else can you shoot dozens of people you don't know?"

James Holmes was another example of a very gifted young man who allowed his obsession with fantasy games and role-play to eclipse the real world and this led to schizophrenia taking hold. Yes, there were all the usual warning signs, but as we saw in chapter 2, the pseudocommando often kills indiscriminately and in broad daylight. Holmes actions were in that sense, unpredictable, except perhaps to a clinical psychologist. Holm, in fact, was being treated by such a professional.

Dr Lynn Fenton, a Psychiatrist working for the University of Colorado, was approached by Campus Police who became alarmed at Holmes bizarre behavior. During a session with Dr. Fenton, Holmes had told of his fantasies about killing a lot of people.

Compulsion To Kill

She was therefore well aware of the problems. The Campus police offered to place him under a psychiatric hold for 72 hours.

Dr Fenton rejected the idea. Holmes' name was, however brought to the attention of the university's Behavior Evaluation and Threat Assessment team or BETA for short. A flow chart released by the university shows guidelines for action that could be followed if a person is deemed a direct threat. This would have included detention for assessment but it did not happen. At the time of this writing, further records have been withheld under a gag order while lawyers argue for more disclosures.

During my years in law enforcement, if I learned anything, it was, never try to out guess the jury in a legal case. Therefore, I will refrain from any further speculation but having caught him at the scene, the police have overwhelming evidence that Holmes committed the crime. The only question left is his mental state. As with all shootings the inevitable cries for gun control started before the bodies had even been removed.

Personally, I do not subscribe to further gun control, but aside from that I have a question to those who look for simple solutions.

Compulsion To Kill

Who was to blame for these killings, Remington, Ruger, or Smith and Wesson who made the weapons, The Campus Police, The Theatre Management?

Or was it maybe a mentally disturbed ex-student wanting to ensure he exacted revenge on a world he had perceived was out to destroy him.

Compulsion To Kill

Compulsion To Kill

Chapter 4

<u>MEDICAL DIAGNOSIS</u>

As we have seen, the process that turns seemingly normal well-adjusted young men into mass killers is not an easy path to follow. There are however many factors that link these random Acts. The pseudocommando does not always follow a set of rules. Neither do all traits apply to all killers. But most are lonely individuals and are pre-occupied by the fantasy world of video games and role-play. This of course applies to many other teenagers, (some would say all), but they do not go on to become killers. If they did then we would be neck high in bodies.

Something else triggers them. Broadly psychiatrists define these traits as schizophrenia and Paranoia.

Symptoms of Schizophrenia

Schizophrenia symptoms normally develop slowly over months or even years. Sometimes a subject may have multiple symptoms, and at other times only a handful.

Compulsion To Kill

However, some symptoms are common to all types of schizophrenia.

The three main categories of the illness are,

Paranoid schizophrenia

A condition that is associated with anger and/or an irrational fear that someone or something is out to harm you or your family.

Disorganized schizophrenia

Childlike behavior, problems thinking and explaining your ideas clearly. They exhibit little or no emotion.

Catatonic schizophrenia

Irresponsive to others, generally inactive and adopting a rigid posture, often exhibiting bizarre behavior such as facial contortions and pained expressions.

****

Let us look more closely at Paranoid schizophrenia, as this is the condition that is most closely associated with the mass killers.

Compulsion To Kill

The classic features of paranoid schizophrenia are having delusions and hearing things that aren't real.

This is the classic voices in my head, excuse; paranoid schizophrenia is a serious condition that lasts a lifetime. It can be controlled by medication but it can never be completely cured, complications can lead to suicidal behavior and may also be the trigger for something altogether more sinister.

It is true that the ability to control memory and emotions may not seem as important as compared with other forms of the illness, but that does not make it less severe. In fact it is more likely to lead to a false sense of security. Family and friends may not see a problem and deduce that.

'Johnny is just a little eccentric, these days'

Well he may be, but that eccentric behavior may be masking something more serious. If correctly diagnosed, the condition can be effectively controlled and this is the case in most patients. However, this is not the case with the lonely single man who keeps to himself, rarely interacts with people of his own age, and is preoccupied with pastimes like video or computer games. He is also the one most likely to slip under the radar.

Compulsion To Kill

If there is no close friends or family to observe him on a day-to-day basis, then there is, in effect no monitoring.

Certainly, killers like Tucson shooter Jared Lee Loughner are able to cut their medication and allow the schizophrenia to take control. Likewise with the Aurora cinema shooter James Holmes, who was undergoing treatment from a college psychiatrist for the same condition before he dropped out, and the file was closed.

The unfortunate truth here is that all of us exhibit some of the symptoms of schizophrenia at some time or another in our lives. If we are angry with our spouse or boss, if we feel that they just don't get it. If we enjoy playing the occasional computer game or, sometime we just need to be alone, does that make us all potential killers? Of course not, but it does illustrate very clearly how difficult it is to diagnose the condition unless we have special psychiatric skills.

For this reason it is unwise to go too far down the path of amateur psychoanalysis. The human mind is a very deep pit of elaborate emotions and feelings, of passions of love and hate, pride and regrets. No human beings are exactly alike; we share many traits and have many differing views.

Compulsion To Kill

We have established a set of rules and standards that most of us can agree upon. We have a general sense of what is right and wrong, but we hold different views on exactly what is right and wrong.

Some of us justify breaking the law; if we feel that the law itself is wrong. We look to a higher sometimes-religious definition. Some of us would say that we all have a right to life, so does that also mean we have the right to take life in order to preserve other lives. If so what about the lives we take, do they forfeit the right to life, and who are we to make that decision?

OK! Now we can see that the mental state of each of us is extremely difficult, if not impossible to comprehend. Our top Psychiatrists are able to comprehend some of its workings but most would tell you, that anyone who states he completely understands the human mind is a liar.

Perhaps the answer is that we all need order in our lives and such questions can be safely put aside if we can only say,

Well I may not agree with it personally but the law is the law. So we can move on.

At this point the reader may think I am offering excuses for the horrendous crimes of these killers.

Compulsion To Kill

That is not the case, but simply arresting, trying, and maybe executing the perpetrators has not stopped them from occurring. That is probably because there is no deterrent factor that would break through the mental cage around the mind of a paranoid killer.

Most do not expect to survive the incident anyway, so thoughts of punishment and retribution are the least of their concerns.

Therefore it must fall upon the rest of us to look for answers. In doing so, we may discover a common trait or link that will sound an alarm.

In the 21 years that I served as a police officer, I met many criminals who had committed inexplicable crimes. From the young girl who smashed a shop window to steal a bag of cat litter (she did not own a cat); to a teenage schoolboy who had suddenly strangled an old lady he was visiting, for no conceivable reason.

These people were certainly disturbed. In the case of the latter, although I was not directly involved in the investigation, I did get the opportunity to speak to him while escorting him to a detention center. What struck me and my colleagues was just how ordinary this boy seemed.

Compulsion To Kill

There was nothing abnormal about him; I listened while he spoke to his father about looking after his pets and how his schoolwork was progressing. This was a normal young schoolboy with the same aspirations and hopes as any other. What made him different was a sudden act of mindless violence.

At another time, I was escorting a female prisoner, who had been committed to a mental unit; I was sitting in the rear seat behind the driver with her sitting alongside me. This was standard procedure when transporting prisoners. The journey was uneventful with the prisoner chatting about her life and how stupid she felt about what she had done.

I remember telling her that this was just an assessment and, that no one condemned her for making a mistake. As we turned into the entrance to the hospital, a glazed look came over her eyes and she suddenly became extremely violent, kicking out at the driver and screaming obscenities. The change was instantaneous and extremely alarming. It took a great deal of effort to restrain her, and the driver did well to keep control of the car. Hospital staff subdued her.

Compulsion To Kill

Sociopathic

Another psychological disorder, often associated with the mass shooter is Sociopathy, also known as Antisocial Personality Disorder or psychopathy.

Individuals with this disorder have little regard for the feeling and welfare of others. As a clinical diagnosis it is usually limited to those over age 18.

It can however be professionally diagnosed in younger people if the they commit isolated antisocial acts while showing no signs of any another mental disorder.

Antisocial Personality Disorder is a chronic illness, beginning in adolescence and continuing throughout adulthood. There are ten generally recognized symptoms

1. The inability to learn from experience.

2. A total lack of responsibility.

3 An inability to control impulses.

4. A lack of moral sensibility.

5. Severe anti-social behavior.

6. No change in behavior following punishment.

Compulsion To Kill

7. Emotional immaturity.

8. An absence of any feeling of guilt or remorse.

9. Self-centeredness.

10 An inability to form any meaningful
relationship.

Patients who suffer with this disorder may also
exhibit criminal behavior. They are frequently
unemployed or if they do work, are frequently
absent or may quit suddenly, with no apparent
reason.

They show a marked lack of consideration to other
people's wishes, welfare, or rights. They can be
manipulative and may frequently lie to gain
personal pleasure or profit.

Other symptoms include defaulting on loans,
failure to provide child support, or failing to care
for their dependents adequately.

High-risk sexual behavior and drug abuse are other
common traits of this condition.

Compulsion To Kill

Impulsive behavior failure to plan ahead, aggressiveness, noticeable irritability, irresponsible behavior and a reckless disregard for their own safety and/or the safety of others are traits of the antisocial personality.

Males are more likely to be antisocial than females. Those from the lower socioeconomic groups are more susceptible.

When reviewing this list, many of us may identify some of these traits in ourselves, in an assessment from a manager or simple accusations raised in a domestic argument between partners. Therein lays the difficulties faced by the mental health professional. If the reader understands that, then they are well on the way to appreciating the complexity of the problem. There are many theories about the cause of Antisocial Personality Disorder but little consensus. Other factors that may provide a trigger are, neglectful parenting as a child, low levels of certain neurotransmitters in the brain, and a general belief that antisocial behavior can be justified when difficult circumstances are present.

Psychotherapy, group therapy, is a recognized common treatment. However it is an unfortunate fact that most people with Antisocial Personality Disorder reject treatment. Therefore results are inconclusive and recovery rates are low.

Compulsion To Kill

The notion that all sociopaths are very clever is a myth. Many are failures who make others suffer for their inadequacies. Most sociopaths are profoundly chaotic types.

Compulsion To Kill

Compulsion To Kill

Above: Bath school after the explosion.

Above Left: Explosives removed from the school by law enforcement officers following the blast. **Above Right:** Andrew Kehoe, the first suicide bomber, Car bomber and   the biggest mass killer of schoolchildren in US History.

Compulsion To Kill

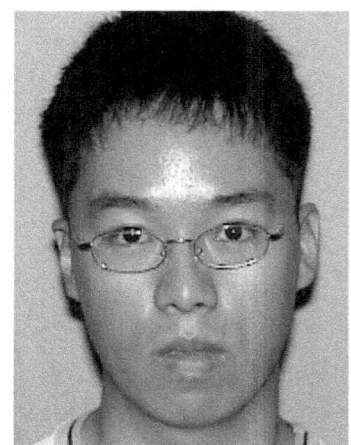

Above Left: Sandy Hook killer Adam Lanza.

Above Right: Seng hui Cho (Virginia State Police picture). Two disturbed young men who grew up to become mass shooters of 1st grade and High school children, respectivly.

Above Left: Columbine Killer Dylan Klebold.

Above Right: Aurora shooter James Holmes.

Compulsion To Kill

Two killers, whose schizophrenia and Video game addiction set them on a course to live out their fantasies in a hail of murderous fire on their unarmed victims.

(All pictures public domain)

Above: Tucson, AZ shooter Jared Longner gives a chilling stare in his mugshot that only hints at the madness that drove him to shoot Congresswoman Gabrial Giffords and many of her supporters in a frenzy of shooting.

Compulsion To Kill

Above: Killer Pekka-Eric Auvinen, posted these pictures on the internet shortly before the killings, dressed in the same t-shirt and with the gun he used in the mass killings.

Above: Security cameras at Columbine High School capture Dylan Klybold and Eric Harris in the school Cafeteria. (Columbine High School)

Compulsion To Kill

Above: A candlelight vigil at Virginia Tech after the massacre.

Above: Police issued this later mug shot of Holmes .He has lost the orange hair but not the chilling stare.

Compulsion To Kill

Above: Dave Coustick's picture of Dunblane Primary School, Scotland.

Above: The Century 16 cinema complex in Aurora Co. shortly after the shooting.

Compulsion To Kill

Above: Police cordon off Adam Lanza,s car on the day of the shootings.

All pictures on this and previous pages are public domain .

Compulsion To Kill

Chapter 5

THE ROLE OF THE MEDIA

The United States is a less violent country than it was two decades ago. The homicide rate, which hit a peak in the early 1990s at about 10 per 100,000 people, has been cut in half to a level not seen since the early 1960s. This statistic alone should surprise everyone who believes we live in a very violent country. But there is more, gun ownership in the USA has risen sharply, particularly in the last 3 years, official estimates show that it has risen 20%, from 80 million to 100 million. This may be due to a fear among the populace, of rising crime or greater publicity, or it may simply be a result of a fear that Congress would tighten gun control or eliminate gun ownership altogether. Both have so far been proved wrong.

The reasons for the increase in gun ownership are difficult to pin down. Few independent statistics are available. Here in Kentucky, the State tops the whole country for gun sales, yet we are not the largest or the most populace. Neither are we known for violent crime. We are a quiet law abiding community. So! What is going on? Students that attend our concealed carry classes usually say the reason is the wish to feel secure and be able to defend themselves.

Compulsion To Kill

Contact that we have with other instructors and other firearms schools, tell a similar story. But if you follow the news through the various media outlets you get a far different picture.

The media generally portray America as a violent society where guns are the first means used to settle arguments, where gunfights are as common as those on the old TV westerns.

But this is a false idea. The country gets to know about a violent incident through the media. And therefore the media have the power to publicize or bury any incident as they think fit. A clear illustration of this was the shooting in Florida of a black teenager Trayvon Martin by neighborhood watch volunteer George Zimmerman in 2012. The media elevated the incident to such proportions that no lesser person than The President of the United States got involved, and the Justice Dept. sent a special prosecutor to take over the investigation, resulting in the Police Chief that was leading the investigation, having little choice but to stand down.

We saw the rise of extreme groups like the Black Panthers marching in support of black power and death threats against Zimmerman, who was forced into hiding with his family. We saw normally levelheaded journalists go overboard to demonize both Zimmerman and his family.

Compulsion To Kill

At the same time heavy media coverage dwelt on the grieving family of the slain teenager. So why did this one incident cause so much upheaval, to the point that all other world events were pushed into the background?

Most of this was driven by the left wing of the media who have long wanted to stop the issue of concealed carry permits and generally bring in severe restrictions on gun ownership. An example of how this can be done was seen in the selective editing of "911" calls released at the time and rebroadcast from news outlets like NBC news, tending to show Zimmerman had a racial motive. Example; when the dispatcher asked Zimmerman if the suspect was black or white, Zimmerman replied

"I think he's black. "

The dispatchers question was edited out and the answer blended to the initial call. So that Zimmerman appeared to say he was following a black man. This sort of fraudulent reporting was rife and together with other manufactured statements, added to the wealth of misinformation regarding the case.

The facts of the case were forgotten as spin after spin was put on the story.

Compulsion To Kill

Within Days the incident was being portrayed as a white vigilante hunting down and murdering an unarmed black youth, whose only crime was being black. Left wing Democrats in Congress joined in the clamor. The "911" tapes from other witnesses, together with any other evidence that supported Zimmerman's claim of self-defense were totally ignored. Even when the evidence surfaced of Zimmerman's injuries and medical reports of his treatment were released, the media by and large ignored it.

Photos circulated of the slain teenager were old high school images; newer images were available but were never used. To do so would tarnish the image of the innocent high school victim shot down in cold blood. There is an old saying, that truth is the first casualty of war. In the war of the ratings it appears no different.

The media had staked everything on their version of what happened, and were never going to admit wrongdoing. Although NBC was forced to apologize for the editing of the "911" tapes, which they blamed on an error, it is hard to believe when taken in context with their overall handling of the case. The damage was done. Later a wealth of confidential evidence on the case was *"inadvertently":* leaked to the press by the prosecution. This included Zimmerman's school reports grades and a photo of Martins corpse taken shortly after the shooting.

Compulsion To Kill

To the independent observer, this illustrated the desperation of the prosecution, as their case began to collapse. At the time of this writing it remains to be seen if Zimmerman will get a fair trial but it appears that the media will do everything in their power to prevent it.

Contrast that with the following incident.

On Sunday May 25, 2008 at approximately 2:30 a.m. Ernesto Fuentes Villagomez, age 30 of Winnemucca, entered a bar in Winnemucca, Nevada and opened fire in the crowded bar, killing two patrons and wounding 2 others before a 48 year old concealed carry permit holder drew his own gun and shot the killer dead. The Nevada police did not release the name of the man who had undoubtedly stopped a massacre. No charges were filed. The media of course quickly buried the story; after all they cannot allow people to think that some killings can be curtailed by an armed citizen who can return fire.

This incident was completely ignored with all major news outlets refusing to cover it. The fact that the name of the armed citizen was withheld also helped the cover up. The media simply said the item was not newsworthy. The killer was Hispanic, and that fact did not go well with the left, who would have preferred a white tea party man.

Compulsion To Kill

No mileage in vilifying a Hispanic, heaven forbid, the public ever get the idea that mass killers may not all be right wing white conservatives.

So! Faced with this sort of media bias, the American public are, understandably confused. The TV stations tell them that gun crime is rampant and that the NRA is the purveyors of death. They state categorically that our gun laws are leading to whole scale murder. They constantly preach that the country would be far safer without guns.

However, the statistics and data available from the FBI, Law enforcement, and independent surveys indicate exactly the opposite. Murders are actually well down. The states with the strictest gun control also have the highest murder rates. Despite this, the mayor of Chicago, Rahm Emanuel continues to advocate gun bans in a state that has the strictest gun control in the country and a murder rate off the scale. (275 between Jan 1st and July 20th 2012).

So let us do something radical here, Let us speculate, that to test the theory, a US city decided that, instead of imposing gun control they would pass a law that compelled everyone to own a gun and be competent in its use. What would be the result? Mayhem? Mass murder? Crime through the roof?

Compulsion To Kill

Well actually we do not need to speculate. There is a town in the USA that did precisely that. Kennesaw, Georgia, a city with a population of 29,784 people that was recently selected by Family Circle as one of America's 10 Best Towns for Families.

Back in 1982, Kennesaw did the opposite of what most cities do. Not only did it not outlaw or restrict guns, but it actually passed a law requiring that every head of household in town own a handgun, and be competent in its use. (With exceptions for criminal record, religious objection, handicap, etc.)

Contrary to hysterical predictions from the left wing media groups and anti-gun groups, there was no bloodbath, no rise in violence, in fact crime figures plunged and have stayed low.

In fact, there are thousands of cases in the US, daily, where armed citizens stop crime or murders. Most go unreported nationally, and often only warrant a 10-second slot on the local news. A search on U tube will bring up some gleaned from security cameras. And the NRA monthly publications do list some of the events with brief details. But overall there is little appetite for the media to report such incidents which would severely discredit their Anti – Gun Stance.

Compulsion To Kill

So what figures can we trust?

In May 2011 the FBI released preliminary figures with relation to gun and violent crime. They do not make good reading for the advocates of gun control.

In 2010 violent crime in the USA decreased by 6% to a 37 year low. Green Bay Wisconsin led the way with a 22% reduction followed by El Paso, Texas with a 58% decrease in murders over 2009.

A notable exception was NYC, which with its restrictive gun laws recorded a 14% increase in the murder rate. With the forced repeal of anti gun laws in Washington DC, they recorded as expected a slight reduction in murder rates with DC and Chicago recording a reduction of 6% and 8% respectively. This following the overturning of the most stringent anti- gun laws, following the Supreme Court Heller decision that affirmed the right to keep and bear arms applied to all citizens.

The same time as crime decreased, firearms ownership increased. FBI national criminal background checks, the majority of which are for firearms purchase, hit an all-time high of 14 million. At the National Rifle Association's Conference in St Louis in 2012, the figures given following the latest survey showed approximately one hundred million gun owners in the USA.

Compulsion To Kill

Faced with figures like this and knowing that gun owners are also voters, is it surprising that the United States Congress and the Obama administration were unwilling to move forward on gun control.
Maybe there is truth in the old adage, don't believe everything you read in the newspapers.

Notably at the time of writing, July 2012, Illinois is the only State that does not allow the issue of concealed carry permits. Its crime is predictably extremely high. As criminals are in effect lawbreakers and therefore do not follow gun laws, the concealed carry ban ensures the criminal gunman that there is little chance of him facing an armed response. These are the facts.

They are available on line and prove that far from being a problem, lawful gun ownership keeps crime low and citizens safer. Following the Aurora cinema shooting of July 2012, the pro gun lobby hit out at the fact that the cinema operated a no gun policy, therefore making it unlikely that the killer would face any opposition.

Since the dawn of the television age, parents, teachers, legislators, not to mention mental health professionals have been concerned about the content of television programs and its impact, particularly on children. Of special concern has been the portrayal of violence on screen.

Compulsion To Kill

In 1982, research was carried out by The National Institute of Mental Health to try and identify the link between violence among children and that depicted on TV. The results were startling.

1. Children became less sensitive to the pain and suffering of others.
2. Children may become more fearful of the world around them.
3. Children may be more likely to behave in an aggressive or harmful way towards others.

As a result of 15 years of consistently disturbing findings about the violent content of children's programs, the Surgeon General's Scientific Advisory Committee on Television and Social Behavior was formed in 1969 to assess the impact of violence on the attitudes, values, and behavior of viewers. The resulting Surgeon General's report and a follow-up report in 1982:

Research by psychologists L. Rowell Huesmann, Leonard Eron and others found that children who watched many hours of violence on television when they were in elementary school tended to also show a higher level of aggressive behavior when they became teenagers.

Compulsion To Kill

By observing these youngsters into adulthood, Drs. Huesmann and Eron found that the ones who'd watched a lot of TV violence when they were eight years old were more likely to be arrested and prosecuted for criminal acts as adults. Interestingly, being aggressive as a child, did not predict watching more violent TV as a teenager, suggesting that TV watching may more often be a cause rather than a consequence of aggressive behavior.

This is a disturbing revelation. It has been known for a while, in fact ever since psychologist Albert Bandura's excellent work on social learning and the tendency of children to imitate what they see, proved what any parent could have told him. Children copy by example, especially when they are young. Of course no one has suggested that every child watching Miami Vice will become a mass murderer, but some children are more impressionable than others, when killing becomes the norm, children will become desensitized to it. And that can never be a good thing.

Violent video games are a more recent phenomenon, or at least more so than TV and films. Therefore there has been less research on their effects.

Compulsion To Kill

However, that done by psychologist Craig A. Anderson and others does show that playing violent video games can increase a person's aggressive thoughts, feelings, and behavior both in laboratory settings and in actual life. In fact, a study by Dr. Anderson in the year 2000 suggests that violent video games may be more harmful than violent television and movies because they are interactive, very engrossing and require the player to identify with the aggressor.

This is not to suggest that video games themselves are a bad thing, it is known they can be a useful tool in sharpening skills of co-ordination and target identification. This is precisely why video simulators are used by law enforcement and the Secret Service. Some like Silent Scope and the old favorites, Duck and Crow Hunter are useful in honing skills of target identification. In fact the US Military took the game duck hunt and reprogrammed it substituting targets and weapons to produce their own version, named MACS which stood for Multipurpose Arcade Combat Simulator, (doesn't the government just love these mnemonics) the game was more popularly known by the troops as the Nintendo Game.

Compulsion To Kill

Currently the US military uses similar arcade style simulators to teach marksmanship. They did this after noting that certain child killers had a kill ratio (Number of kills per shot) of close to 100%, far better than the average combat soldier.

There are of course dangers, most soldiers played video games before joining up, and this does not seem to have harmed them. There are psychological pressures on the armed forces and many do suffer from Post Traumatic Stress and other issues. But these have always been apparent in the combat soldier, in the Civil War, WW1, WW2, and Korean Conflicts that were played out long before the inventions of the computer and its associated video game era.

In his book "On Combat" (warrior press) Lt Col Dave Grossman observes that. .

"When kids use these games, they are not just murder simulators but mass murder simulators. Is there a kid anywhere in the world who puts his coins into a video game machine, picks up a realistic gun, shoots only one virtual person, puts it down and walks away? No they are trained to kill all the virtual people and rack up a high score."

Compulsion To Kill

Dr. Anderson and other researches are also looking into how violent music lyrics affect children and adults. In a 2003 study involving college students, Anderson found that songs with violent lyrics increased aggression related thoughts and emotions and this effect was directly related to the violent content of the lyrics. "One major conclusion from this and other research on violent entertainment media is that "content matters," says Anderson. " This message is important for all consumers, but especially for parents of children and adolescents."

All involved in the media have an effect on how we view violence and our understanding of it.

The average American child watches 8,000 made for television murders and 100,000 acts of violence, by the time they finish grade school. The number will have doubled by the time they graduate from High school.

The alarming statistics have not fallen on deaf ears; in 1969 the Milton Eisenhower Commission reported, "We are deeply troubled by the televisions constant portrayal of violence in pandering to a public pre-occupation with violence that television itself has helped to generate."

A further study in 1992 made a plea for a sane program of internal regulation and self-restraint.

Compulsion To Kill

This too was ignored. Faced with a ratings war and the public's appetite for graphic depictions of violence we saw the emergence of more and more blood and gore on our screens.

Was it wise for the American people to disregard the warning signs? And if they did so, by ignoring the warnings where would that lead?

The answer can be found at Columbine, Virginia Tech, and Jonesboro. If we are constantly teaching our kids to kill, either by accident or neglect, the adolescent who spends most of his down time in front of a video screen and building up a huge body count is slowly conditioning themselves. Can we really be surprised when they learn how to kill, and later pass the test with flying colors?

Compulsion To Kill

Compulsion To Kill

Chapter 6

<u>MASS SHOOTINGS IN EUROPE</u>

If you were to believe all that is written about mass school shootings, you could be forgiven for thinking that all of them occur within the United States and that it is a unique problem directly linked to America's gun ownership. Well! Although the US leads the tables in this sort of crime we are by no means the only country to have this problem. Also of the world's countries, we are one of the largest. Data on this sort of crime is not really available from China and the former Soviet Union. And only major events like the one at Beslan get publicity, and then it is usually heavily censored and only available after much gerrymandering by the authorities.

Europe however is more open. On September 23rd 2008 a shooting occurred at the Kauhajoki School of hospitality at the Seinäjoki University of applied Sciences in Western Finland.

Twenty Two (22) year old Matti Juhani Saari was born on May 20th 1986. He was a hospitality management student on a degree course at the time of the shooting.

Compulsion To Kill

On entering the school, Saari initially opened fire on a group of students taking an exam on business studies, then he entered at least one other classroom where he continued shooting. According to accounts from three students who were able to escape the exam room, Saari had approached his victims individually before shooting them. It was also said that he was reveling in the situation and was acting very aggressively. In an adjacent classroom, student Sanna Orpana, said that her class had heard "shooting and a kind of a rumble like tables falling down." She believed at the time that the noise may have been coming from a toy gun, and two other students went to investigate the noise. Saari immediately opened fire on them and the remaining students in Orpana's classroom hid under a table, before running upstairs.

As with similar incidents in the US, Saari encountered little resistance, and the massacre was concluded relatively quickly. The killer having run out of targets, and then covered the classroom in a flammable liquid, believed to be petrol, and set the room ablaze. Saari then encountered Jukka Forsberg, the schools caretaker, and fired several shots at him but missed. He then shot out all the windows in the main corridor, firing some shots into the air. Later Forsberg stated the gunman was very well prepared. He walked calmly and seemed well aware of his actions.

Compulsion To Kill

At around 11 a.m. the first police units arrived on scene. A police van with two officers entered the yard of the college where they were shot at by Saari and forced to retreat. Further units arrived including an armored car. However, in the confusion and fire diversions Saari managed to escape. Two days after the killings, a friend of Saari's, named Rauno, called the police to say that at 11:53 he had received a call from Saari, in which he confessed to having killed ten people. He is claimed to have spoken to Rauno in a calm manner, telling him that he wanted to say goodbye. The Police immediately rushed to the address where they found Saari alive, having shot himself in the head. He was taken to Tampere University Hospital, where he was treated but to no avail and he died a short time later. Only 10 students died, despite the fact that over 100 shots were fired.

The incident was the second school shooting in less than a year in Finland. The other being the Jokela School Shooting in November 2007, in which nine people including the gunman were killed. The circumstances of the incident are as follows.

At approximately 11:40 a.m. 18-year-old student Pekka-Eric Auvinen entered the school's main hallway at the High school in Jokela, a small town located in the municipality of Tuusula, Finland.

Compulsion To Kill

The gunman was armed with a. 22 sig Mosquito semi -automatic pistol. Without warning he opened fire on the helpless students.

The emergency services received the first phone call at 11:43. At 11:44, the school Principal Helena Kalmi ordered all students and teachers to barricade themselves inside their classrooms. The brave woman then left the school administration office and tried to convince Auvinen to surrender. The crazed killer was unmoved, and shot her seven times in full view of a group of students in the schoolyard, killing her instantly.

Auvinen then began walking around the school, knocking on classroom doors. He shouted orders at some of the students, proclaimed a revolution, and urged the students to destroy school property. He also aimed his weapon at some people without shooting them. Others he shot apparently at random, including the school nurse who was attempting to care for the wounded. The victims all sustained multiple injuries to the upper body and head area. He later began pouring two-stroke engine fuel on corridor walls and floors, but for some reason he was fortunately not able to ignite the fuel.

A police patrol vehicle arrived at 11:55, followed later by about one hundred police officers at about 12:30, including the Police special operations unit.

Compulsion To Kill

Even off-duty police officers arrived and surrounded the school. When the police tried to negotiate with Auvinen, he fired a shot at the police. The shooting spree ended after 40 minutes when Auvinen shot himself in the head.

The police entered the school at 13:53. They found Auvinen in a boys' lavatory with a self-inflicted head wound. He was still alive but unconscious at 13:54. The police searched one room at a time for other shooters. The police were not able to secure the building until shortly before 16:00. None of the police officers fired their weapons.

Auvinen was taken to the Töölö Hospital of the Helsinki University Central Hospital at 14:45 where he died at 22:15 from the self-inflicted gunshot wound.

Compulsion To Kill

Pekka-Eric Auvinen

Auvinens Sig Mosquito. 22

Compulsion To Kill

So! Why is it that the general media outlets in the USA, tend to downplay or even ignore shootings overseas. The reason is mostly political. The majority of the media coverage of shootings here is driven by the anti gun lobby, and most anchors and reporters tend to put an anti gun slant on the report.

Usually, you see interviews with representatives from the gun control organizations, such as the Brady Group and Mayors against illegal guns.

Many interviews with victims and their families are all good fuel for their agenda, which rarely backfires. One time it did was when they interviewed Suzanna Hupp who had just seen her parents shot down by a crazed gunman in Luby's bar in Texas. Unexpectedly, Ms Hupp, a concealed carry permit holder blamed the lawmakers who had prevented her from carrying a gun in their self-appointed gun free zones. Ms Hupp later became a State legislator and successfully overturned the law. She continues to be a stalwart defender of gun rights.

These media groups rarely interview NRA or gun rights groups, but usually read an edited statement from them.

Compulsion To Kill

The problem with such a one sided campaign is that no one looks for the real reasons why such shooting's occur. It seems easier to blame the guns than the perpetrator.

That avoids facing unpleasant questions about how we deal with mentally ill individuals and how we regulate on line video distributors and the violence culture that they portray. There does appear to be a link with all these shooters and we will explore that in a later chapter.

Chapter 7

<u>SO! WHY WASN'T ANYTHING DONE?</u>

That is the question seemingly every media commentator asks following a mass shooting. It was echoed at Tucson and Aurora. And often criticism is leveled at the police, social services, and mental health authorities. As we saw in the chapter on the media, we need to analyze first, the motive for the media asking such a question? What sounds like an attempt to tune into the outrage felt around the country is in fact a smokescreen. The prime reason a TV station or Newspaper exists is to make money. In order to get revenue they need to become well known, even controversial. The seeds are set for reports to be slanted in such a way that people will tune in. The truth or otherwise of the report takes secondary importance to its believability.

As a former police officer I always looked at crimes from a legal point of view. A police officer who allows his own feelings or views to override the legal implications is set to, at best, lose his case, or at worst face charges himself. The media however have different criteria.

Compulsion To Kill

In this society of political correctness and over regulation, the social worker or police officer who suspects a person may not be *'Quite Right'!,* is in a real dilemma. Does talking about violence and having an interest in guns, make a person likely to become a mass killer?

At what point does a passion for video games become an obsession with killing?

We must accept that what seems odd behavior to us may be perfectly acceptable to others.

For example, I recall a case a few years back where a police officer was asked to interview an applicant for a firearm certificate. The officer recommended, following the interview, that the application be refused. It was, and the applicant appealed.

At the subsequent hearing, the Police officer testified that he was uneasy about the applicant's mental state. He based this on his observations that the applicant had several gun books and magazines in view, which indicated to him an obsession with guns.

The applicant won his case, but the incident showed a fatal flaw in allowing Police Officers or other officials, with no knowledge or interest in guns, to make judgments on those whose interest lies in that direction.

Compulsion To Kill

If an interest in guns makes the authorities suspicious, then what about re-enactors re-fighting historical battles. Do they not also show an indulgence of fantasy violence?

Where in fact, do we draw lines, and who should draw them?

When the issue of shotgun certificates became law in the UK, the Home Office decreed that any application had to be countersigned by a doctor attesting that the applicant was of sound mind and temperate habits. Well! Sounds good in practice and I am sure many in the Brady camp would applaud. Predictable few doctors would agree to sign, as they knew that mental illness development in the future is impossible to predict. A fact overlooked by the Home Office who were generally against private gun ownership. There is a general suspicion, not without foundation in the US that concerns about the prevention of these killings is really a smokescreen to pass stricter gun control. The ultimate aim from the liberal left of the political spectrum is a total ban, similar to that in the UK. There is a rift developing in the country that threatens to split the country into two separate camps. Those that support the US constitution as written and believe all laws made under it are inviolate. And those that want to change and modify the US society.

Compulsion To Kill

The latter do not only want the Second Amendment abolished, they are also fighting to redefine the entire Constitution, with proposals to remove the whole concept of one nation under God.

We see it in efforts to re-define marriage and repeal all immigration laws. And we see it in attempts to redefine the right to keep and bear arms. A simple amendment that means exactly what it says. The writer, James Madison defined in several federalist papers exactly what it means and this is why the Supreme Court has constantly upheld it.

On the other side there are the supporters of traditional American values, who believe in the pledge that states One Nation, under God, indivisible, with liberty and justice for all.

On the face of it, these two camps will never resolve their differences. At the time of this writing these arguments are being resolved in court hearings, but how long before they degenerate into violence.

So! To return to the question at the start of this chapter; Nothing was done because no one foresaw the incidents before they happened. Most parents see no harm in fantasy computer games that keep their kids out of the way in their bedrooms, out of trouble.

Compulsion To Kill

They do not react kindly to being told that their kids may likely become psychopaths.

It is however true that today's society has changed out of all recognition, compared to the 50s and 60s. The advent of social media, laptops, and cell phones has totally transformed the way that our world operates.

The development of the internet has changed forever the way we educate our children and how we disseminate information.

Gone are the one to one conversations between teachers and pupils parents and children, long distance on-line learning is the norm. Dangers also stalk the internet and our education system.

With no coherent standards between states or sometimes-even cities, we have both Left and Right wing academics pushing their own brand of education on their charges. These ideas can range from Atheism and Racism to Marxism and holocaust denial. Later this imbalance in the teaching doctrine emerges on both sides of the political spectrum.

Role models of yesteryear Lucille Ball and the Walton's have been replaced with Rappers screaming hate songs and anti-hero's like Rambo killing everyone they disagree with.

Compulsion To Kill

Is it then any wonder that, while growing up, our children lose their way and have difficulty in separating fantasy from reality?

The Media have a responsibility to all of us, to ensure they are not shaping the mass killers of tomorrow.

Compulsion To Kill

Chapter 8

<u>SO! WHAT CAN BE DONE?</u>

When a mass shooting like this occurs at a school, there is naturally a clamor for answers on what can and should be done.

Let's deal with the ever-present argument for gun control. Let's visit the gun laws in each State referred to in this book to see the differences.

Colorado

There is no state permit required for the purchase of any rifle, shotgun, or handgun. Firearms dealers are required to keep a record on the retail sale, rental, or exchange of handguns. The record shall include the name of the person to whom the handgun is transferred, his or her age, occupation and residence, and the make, caliber, finish and serial number of the handgun, and the date of the transfer and name of employee making the transfer. The record book shall be open at all times to the inspection of any duly authorized police officer.

Compulsion To Kill

Before a gun show vendor transfers or attempts to transfer a firearm, he or she shall require that a background check, in accordance with the national instant criminal background check system, be conducted of the prospective transferee, and obtain approval of the transfer from the Colorado Bureau of Investigation through a licensed gun dealer.

It is also unlawful to transfer a firearm if any part of the transaction takes place at a gun show, unless a licensed dealer first obtains a background check on the prospective transferee. This does not apply to firearms defined as antiques, curios, or relics under federal law.

A Colorado resident who is otherwise qualified can purchase or receive delivery of a rifle or shotgun in a state contiguous to Colorado, so long as the sale fully complies with the legal conditions of sale in both states and the purchaser and seller have complied with federal law applicable to interstate transactions.

It is unlawful for any person convicted of a felony or conspiracy or attempt to commit a felony, or misdemeanor domestic violence or adjudicated delinquent for a felony to possess a firearm.

It is unlawful for any person under 18 to possess a handgun, and it is unlawful to provide or permit a juvenile to possess a handgun.

Compulsion To Kill

Exceptions include:

- Attendance at a hunter's safety course or firearms safety course.

Connecticut

- A permit is required to carry a handgun on or about one's person, or in a vehicle.
- The applicant must successfully complete a handgun safety course approved by the commissioner.
- A permit may be issued if the issuing authority finds that the applicant "intends to make no use of any pistol or revolver which he may be permitted to carry –other than a lawful use, and is a suitable person."
- Connecticut is in transition from a local permits process to a State Permit Process.
- A statewide permit to carry is valid (unless revoked for cause) for five years.
- A permit to carry may be revoked if the issuing authority determines that the permit holder is no longer a "suitable person" to carry a handgun.

It is unlawful to sell or permanently transfer a handgun to any person who is forbidden to possess a handgun, or to a person under 21.

Compulsion To Kill

No person, firm, or corporation shall sell or transfer any pistol or revolver unless an application provided by the Commissioner of Public Safety is filled out. There is a 2-week waiting period from the date of the application.

A handgun eligibility certificate, valid for five years, shall be issued by the Commissioner of Public Safety within 60 days after receipt of the National Criminal History Records check from the FBI to a person who may lawfully possess a handgun, who completes a handgun safety course, is fingerprinted, and pays a fee.

The eligibility certificate entitles a person to purchase, but not to carry, a handgun.

The commissioner must be notified within two business days of an address change.

The waiting period is waived for police and parole officers, holders of a state permit to carry, holders of a permit to sell handguns, or holders of a handgun eligibility certificate.

Holders of a valid Connecticut hunting license and active or reserve members of the armed forces are also exempt from the waiting period on rifles and shotguns. Antique firearms are exempted from both the waiting period and application form requirements.

Compulsion To Kill

Virginia

A criminal history record information check is required prior to purchasing any firearm, except for an antique or its replica.

A fee of $2.00 will be collected for such a check. For non-residents it is $5.00.

If any buyer or transferee is denied the right to purchase a firearm, he may exercise his right of access to and review of the criminal history record information, provided such action is initiated within thirty days of the denial.

A licensed firearm dealer shall not deliver a rifle or shotgun to a non-resident until an approval report is received from the state police or 10 days have gone by, whichever comes first.

Permit holders may purchase more than 1 handgun a month. Non-licensed persons may only buy 1 handgun a month.

No state permit is required to otherwise purchase or possess a rifle, shotgun, or handgun.

Virginia residents may purchase firearms from any licensed Federal Firearms Licensee, even if they are out of state.

Compulsion To Kill

It is a crime for any person to sell, give, or otherwise furnish a handgun to a minor if he has reason to believe that the buyer or recipient is less than 18 years of age, unless such transfer is made between family members or for the purpose of engaging in a sporting event or activity.

A person under 18 shall not possess or transport a handgun or assault firearm.

This prohibition does not apply to a minor in his own home or on his property or on the property of another with prior permission, while accompanied by an adult while hunting, at a range or firearm educational class, and while transporting an unloaded firearm to and from such activities.

It is unlawful for a person convicted of a felony, or any person under 29 with a juvenile adjudication, as a 14-year-old or older, which would be a felony if committed by an adult, or a person acquitted by reason of insanity and committed to a mental institution, to possess or transport a firearm.

It is unlawful for any person who is subject to a protective order issued pursuant to family abuse or stalking to purchase or transport any firearm while the order is in effect.

Compulsion To Kill

It is unlawful for anyone adjudicated legally incompetent or mentally incapacitated or involuntarily committed to purchase, possess, or transport a firearm. It is unlawful to transfer a firearm to such persons.

It shall be unlawful for any person knowingly to authorize a child under the age of twelve to use a firearm except when the child is under the supervision of an adult.

It is unlawful to possess, sell, transfer, or import any semi-automatic folding stock shotgun with a spring tension drum magazine capable of holding 12 rounds.

As we saw in chapter 1, school killers do not always use guns. Neither do gun control laws prevent shootings such as this one. The gun laws of Connecticut did not deter Adam Lanza from killing 26 people at the Sandy Hook school in Newtown. Any more than strict gun laws of Finland stopped Pekka-Eric Auvinen in his spree there.

In England the severe restrictions on handgun ownership, even before the total ban on handguns did not stop Hamilton's killings there either.

Compulsion To Kill

The gun laws in effect in these locations: Columbine, Virginia Tech, Aurora, Newtown, and the United Kingdom were all different. The shootings were however chillingly similar. So if gun control is not the answer then where else should we look?

School security is one area that is frequently debated. There is merit in the idea that armed police officers at schools may go some way towards deterrence. However this had little effect at Beslan where the armed officer was the first one shot. It is of course true that Beslan was a terrorist event and there were over 30 shooters involved. But nevertheless any school shooter would most likely target the police officer first. Also, cost is always a factor. Could communities afford to place armed police officers or security at every school, to counter a very rare occurrence?

There is of course another way of providing security at no cost, but more of that later.

A third area we could look at is mental evaluation. As we have seen most, if not all shooters suffer from some form of mental imbalance.

This is one area where study and identification of likely suspects is possible, but it is also fraught with pitfalls. If a person is undergoing counseling then the consultations are confidential. They can hardly be otherwise.

Compulsion To Kill

If a doctor was required to inform the police and authorities whenever they were treating a patient, then neither the patient nor their doctor could function effectively. Trust is essential in this type of treatment. We saw in the Aurora shooting that the psychiatrist treating Holms was unable to report her findings outside medical circles, until after his death. The definitions of medical impairment are also open to abuse. We know that the second amendments rights for veterans were denied after some applicants for benefits were adjudicated to be mentally impaired after asking for assistance in filling in forms.

Also, would a health official be prepared to risk a lawsuit from a patient whose confidentiality was breached?

So! To what could be done. Well! As I stated earlier, the strategy should zero in on stopping the would-be killer from entering his target building.

There is an old adage within the firearms community that the only thing capable of stopping a bad man with a gun - is a good man with a gun.

Placing an armed police officer in each school is an attractive idea but impractical. The cost of employing a trained officer, (in reality you would need two to maintain all day coverage,) would be beyond most county budgets.

Compulsion To Kill

How long would county officials continue to maintain this arrangement, 2 years 5, 10? As each year passes with no armed assault the pressure will grow.

A better solution is to arm the staff, this also has problems, but we already have a system of licensed concealed carry holders in every state.

These are individuals who have applied to their State Police for a permit to carry a concealed weapon, usually a handgun on their person.

Such people are required to undergo a training course on the legal use of firearms. They are also required to undergo a stringent background check and prove their competency with a firearm at a live fire exercise supervised by a certified instructor.

There has long been a campaign to allow Concealed Carry permit holders to take their weapons into schools where they are also teachers and staff members. You have to be 21 years of age to obtain such a permit. I favor this approach as a part solution. Of course not all school staff are concealed carry holders and many would not wish to be. So! That is of course their choice. But if they do so, they have to accept that they are increasing the risk of the children in their care.

I also believe that there is a patchwork of laws governing the issue of these permits State by State.

Compulsion To Kill

That means that your concealed carry weapon (CCW) permit holder is not likely to be as well trained in some states as opposed to others.

For instance, many states allow NRA basic pistol instructors to certify CCW courses. The problem here is that the NRA basic pistol course is not a defensive or combat course. It is a Target shooting, gun safety course. Some NRA instructors also have personal protection ratings, including some with the advanced handgun rating, but many do not.

Here in Kentucky we require a marksmanship level to qualify, that consists 4 sets of 5 rounds being fired from a distance of 21 feet (7 yards) at a standard 6 ft Police silhouette target. The applicant is required to hit any portion of the shaded portion 11 time out of 20.

In the two years I have been a certified State instructor I have never had anyone fail. Also, although Kentucky does not accept the NRA rating for instructors (You have to take a Department of Justice approved course,) the course is in my opinion lacking on several points.

There is no required instruction on how to deal with the aftermath of a shooting, deal with the police or prepare mentally for an armed encounter. This is something added as an optional extra by most good instructors.

Compulsion To Kill

If we are to place armed CCW holders in our schools we owe it to both them and the children they are charged with protecting, to ensure that they are all trained to the same standard.

In addition to the armed staff member we need to look at the culture that breeds these killers.

As we have seen, violent video games are part of the culture that our young people indulge in daily. Some spend an abnormal amount of time and money on this activity. On line multi play adds to the mindsets. For commercial reasons, video game manufacturers strive to make games more violent and realistic. The same applies to filmmakers and comic book publishers. To break the fixation will need the combined effort of both the Federal Government and Parents.

The video game ratings should not just be advisory. Laws should be enacted providing strict penalties for dealers selling an 18-rated game to anyone apparently under the age of 18. These penalties should include jail time and loss of trading licenses. Parents who supply or allow such games to be played by young children should not escape sanctions. I would support care orders against such parents, and or fixed penalties, with mandatory jail time for repeat offenders.

Gun control measures would have little effect on stopping such activities.

Compulsion To Kill

Remember that Adam Lanza was banned from purchasing or owning guns. He simply shot his mother with her own gun then took it and four other weapons she owned and used them to massacre all of those innocent children at Newtown, Connecticut in December of 2012.

Will these measures guarantee our children's safety? No! But they will have far greater impact than knee jerk reactions on gun control.

We need to break the hysteria of the gun control media, regarding gun ownership. We need to adopt a mature and responsible attitude to the 2nd Amendment. Statements by New York Mayor Bloomberg, such as those made during the Hurricane Sandy disaster, when he refused all help from the National Guard because he felt the only people allowed to carry guns in his city should be the NYPD. This led to the prolonged suffering of the citizens. Do we really want such people having any say in how to deal with such a serious problem?

Compulsion To Kill

Chapter 9

MOTIVATIONS TO COMMIT MURDER

There are other mass shootings of children and civilians that are not committed by deranged schizophrenics. These are carried out in the name of political ideology. No book on these types of crimes would be complete without a look at these killings. The perpetrators are from a different mold, radical extremism and convince themselves that the cause is worth the carnage and suffering they inflict. However such indifference is not too far removed from the deranged school shooter.

We must go back to the 70s to see the first stirrings of a serious threat to the children of the United States. The Middle East has been a hotbed of insurrection for many years.

The formation of an independent state of Israel in 1948 caused massive resentment in the region with the fledgling state being immediately attacked by its neighbors, determined to achieve by force what they had been unable to at the negotiating table.

What became known as the Arab-Israeli war started off well for the Arab coalition led by Egypt.

Compulsion To Kill

With support from Jordon and Syria the Israeli forces consisted of approximately 29.000 men and a mix of weapons. Arrayed against them was a combined Arab force of 23,000 men from Egypt, Jordon, Iraq, and Syria, plus a few thousand volunteers.

Their forces pressed into Israeli territory but were checked as the Israeli forces regrouped and counter attacked. The war dragged on for a year. By the time an armistice had been signed in 1949, Israel had lost 6,373 men, and the Arabs between 8000 and 15000.

The seeds had been sown for simmering resentment in the region.

Though the war was over the guns did not fall silent. By the end of 1948 the Israeli forces had risen to 108,300. Unable to challenge them personally, embittered Palestinians turned to guerrilla tactics. So began the war of the terrorist which reached its crescendo on September 11th 2001 in New York City.

The **Avivim school bus massacre**

The first attack deliberately targeting children was an attack by the Popular Front for the Liberation Organization General Command (PLOGC) on an Israeli school bus on May 8, 1970.

Compulsion To Kill

It marked a new and frightening campaign by Islamic extremists and one which was destined to be repeated again and again in the following years.

The attack in which 12 Israeli civilians were killed, nine of them children, and 25 were wounded, took place on the road to Moshav Avivim, near Israel's border with Lebanon.

Early in the morning, the bus departed from the town of Avivim heading with its passengers to two local schools. Unknown to the bus's occupants, this route had been scouted by three terrorists, who had slipped over the Border from Lebanon.

A deadly ambush was prepared on the children in the name of Allah.

Ten minutes after leaving Avivim as the bus reached the ambush point two anti tank shells were fired at it using a bazooka, as the bus passed by. The terrorists then opened fire with AK-47 semi automatic weapons from both sides of the road. The driver was among those hit in the initial hail of gunfire as were the two other adults on board.

All three were killed and the bus crashed into an embankment. The attackers continued pouring fire into the vehicle, before fleeing back into Lebanon. The attack was deadly and merciless.

Compulsion To Kill

It also brought the name of "The Popular Front" for the Liberation of Palestine General Command to the front pages of every newspaper in the free world. The attackers were never apprehended.

The children, who were in first to third grade, were buried in a special plot in the Town of Safed, which would again feature in another attack 4 years later.

A monument commemorating the victims of the attack stands in the middle of the Moshav.

- Ester Avikezer, 23
- Yehuda Ohayon, 10
- Yafa Batito, 8
- Mimon Biton, 7
- Haviva Biton, 7
- Chana Biton, 8
- Shimon Biton, 9
- Shulamit Biton, 9
- Machluf Biton, 28
- Aliza Peretz, 14
- Rami Yarkoni, 29
- Shimon Azran, 35

The Popular Front for the liberation of Palestine General Command was founded in 1968 as a splinter group of the Popular Front for the Liberation of Palestine. Both groups were part of the Palestine Liberation Organization (PLO). Although its stated political aim was to create an independent State of Palestine in the Middle East, its actual aim was the destruction of the State of Israel.

Compulsion To Kill

The group was headed by Secretary-General Ahmed Jibril, a former military officer in the Syrian Army who had been one of the PFLP's early leaders. The PFLP-GC declared that its primary focus would be military, not political,

The PFLP-GC maintained cells in several European cities, which carried out anti-American or anti-Israeli operations on behalf of Syria, Libya, and Iran. Jibril remains the leader of the PFLP-GC to this day. The organization is based in Damascus. Since the 1994 Oslo Accord, support for the PFLP-GC has dwindled among Palestinians willing to make concessions to the Jewish state. Currently, the new Palestinian Authority which was formed from an agreement between the PLO and Israel is seen as the best chance of achieving independence. The PFLP-GC is however still very much active and On May 7, 2001, the Israeli seized a Palestinian boat filled with heavy weapons in the port of Haifa. Jibril is widely believed to have been behind the shipment of weapons, which were bound for the Hamas controlled Gaza Strip.

All three groups used terrorism and murder to further their agenda. Mostly, the targets were so called, soft targets such as schools, shopping centers, and restaurants where they could be sure of a high body count with low risk of retaliation.

Compulsion To Kill

<u>The Massacre at Ma'alot</u>

The town of Ma'alot is located six miles from the Lebanese border on a raised plateau in the Israeli province of Western Galilee. On May 15th 1974 this quiet town became synonymous with terrorism at its worst, when three terrorists from the Democratic Front for the Liberation of Palestine (PFLP) crossed the border, intent on murder.

This terror group was a breakaway faction of the PLO (Palestine Liberation Organization.) They were armed with AK-47 automatic rifles, hand grenades, and plastic explosives. They were also dressed in the uniforms of the Israeli Defense Force.
The 3 men Ahmed Lini, Ahmed Haribi, and Zaid Rachim hid until the next night in the orchards near the Druze village of Hurfeish.
An Israeli border patrol unit, later discovered their footprints but could not follow the trail, and mistakenly believed them to be those of smugglers. They reported this to their superiors who did not attach a significantly high priority to the incident.

Meanwhile the terrorists were heading towards the town of Ma'alot. Also, on the same road at this time was a van being driven by a local resident of the town of Hurfeish.

Compulsion To Kill

The vehicle was carrying Christian Arab women home from the village of Fassuta where they worked at a textile works in the Haifa Bay area.

As the van approached, the groups' leader, Ahmed Lini, stepped out into the roadway in front of the vehicle and opened fire.

The bullets from Lini's AK-47 slammed into the van, instantly killing one woman, and wounding both the driver and other workers, one of whom later died of her wounds. The driver, though wounded turned off the headlights and managed to drive backwards up the hill and out of danger.

On reaching Ma'alot, the terrorists knocked on the doors of several homes without answer, but finally reached the home of Fortuna and Yosef Cohen. Unsuspectingly they opened their door. The terrorists immediately shot the couple, killing Yosef, their 4-year old son Eliahu and wounded their 5-year old daughter Miriam.

Fortuna, who was seven months pregnant, tried to flee the intruders, but she was also shot and killed. The only one in the family who survived unhurt was 16-month-old Yitzhak, a deaf-mute, probably because the killers overlooked her. From there, the three terrorists headed for the Netiv Meir Elementary school where students on a school trip were lodging.

Compulsion To Kill

While en route, they met Yaakov Kadosh, a sanitation worker, and asked for directions to the school. They beat and shot him, leaving him for dead.

Netiv Meir elementary school was a three-story concrete building with apartment buildings under construction nearby. The terrorists entered the building at 4 a.m., meeting no resistance from the sleeping children. They initially took 102 students and several teachers hostage. Seventeen students managed to escape by jumping out of windows.

The students were forced to sit on the floor at gunpoint, with explosive charges between them. (This was a scene that would tragically be repeated at a small town in Russia called Beslan, 30 years later in September 2004.)

In the morning, the three terrorists demanded the release from Israeli prisons of 23 Arab and three other prisoners. Unless these conditions were met, they declared that they would kill all the children. They then set deadline for 6:00 p.m. the same day.

At 10 a.m. a young man named Sylvan Zerach, who was at home on leave from the Army, decided to try and get some information on what was gong on in the school.

Compulsion To Kill

He began to climb a water tower not far from the school building to get a closer view of what was going on. He was unfortunately spotted by the terrorists who shot and killed him.

At an emergency session of the Israeli cabinet, a decision was reached to negotiate with the terrorists but the terrorists were in no mood to listen. They turned down a request for more time. The Israelis' had no choice and a call went out to the military.

At 17:25, the commander of the elite Sayeret Matkal Special Forces group was given the 'green light' to storm the building. The commander of the assault force divided his force into three units; two to break in from the entrance while a third was to climb a ladder and enter from a window that faced north. The squads moved into position from the blind side to the east, using the frames of some apartment buildings under construction. The plan called for coordinated simultaneous sniper fire on the three terrorists to hostage-takers. At 17:32 the first squad entered the building through the main entrance on the first floor, which was blocked with tables and chairs. The first three-man team, led by Yuval Galili, was hit by gunfire on the stairs leading to the second floor. Unfazed by his wound, Galili lobbed a phosphorus grenade into the second floor hallway to create a smokescreen.

Compulsion To Kill

Unfortunately, the smoke from the explosion blinded the second assault team led by Amiran Levine, which had been ordered to take out the leader of the group, Ahmed Lini, who was at that time, positioned at the third floor window from where he had shot and killed Zerach.

When they broke into the classroom where the students were being held, Haribi grabbed a student, Gabi Amsalem, and held him at gunpoint on the floor. While Rachim was shot dead, Lini managed to reach the classroom, and grab spare ammunition magazines from the teacher's desk and reload his weapon. He then sprayed the helpless students with machinegun fire and tossed grenades out the window. A burst of Israeli fire broke his left wrist, forcing him to drop his AK-47. In a crazed final act of barbarism he threw two more grenades at a group of girls huddled on the floor. Moments later the mad dog was being cut down by accurate Israeli fire. Meanwhile several more students leaped from the windows to the ground, some ten feet below, as the sound of gunfire filled the school. The elite Israeli force quickly moved through the school. In minutes the operation was over and the three terrorists were dead.

Beside the three terrorists, twenty-two high school students were killed in the senseless attack.

Compulsion To Kill

The student victims were buried in their hometown, Safed. Some of the 10,000 mourners who attended the funerals chanted "Death to the terrorists."

Israel had learned a hard lesson, but it was well learned. Today armed guards are present at all school and school trips and sporting events. There are no gun free zones in Israel and the Islamic terrorists know it. The knowledge that they face certain death is not the deterrent however. Terrorists generally expect to die. What stops their attacks, are the knowledge that they will probably be killed swiftly and without mercy, before they can inflict the planned death toll on their victims.

Beslan

Horrific as the events at Ma'alot were, they paled into insignificance compared to what happened in Russia in 2004.

The First Chechen War was fought from December 1994 to August 1996 between the Russian Federation and the Chechen Republic of Ichkeria, a Sunni Islamic republic which was formerly Soviet territory. The history of which is, to say the least, volatile with constant friction between them and their Russian overlords.

Compulsion To Kill

This stemmed from the forced deportation of most of the population, together with destruction of their buildings and culture, by the Soviet Union following an edict from Josef Stalin.

Their alleged crime? Cooperation with the Nazis during WW2. Although later, the population was allowed back in a piece meal way, relations with Russia never recovered. In 1949 the Soviet authorities erected a statue in the town of Grozny of 19th century Russian general Aleksey Yermolov.

The inscription on the monument did little to endear the people to reconciliation with. It read, "There is no people under the sun more vile and deceitful than this one."

After the initial campaign of 1994–1995, Russian federal forces attempted to seize control of the mountainous area of Chechnya but were set back by Chechen guerrillas, who waged a tenacious hit and run campaign as well as raids on the flatlands.

In spite of Russia's overwhelming firepower and weapons capability, coupled with the fact that the Russian Air Force had total control of the air, the Chechens continued attacks unabated, leading to a widespread demoralization among the troops and an almost total opposition to the war from the Russian public.

Compulsion To Kill

The inevitable ceasefire was signed in 1996 followed by a peace treaty one year later.

The official figure for Russian military deaths is 5,500, while most estimates put the number between 3,500 and 7,500, or even as high as 14,000. Although there are no accurate figures for the number of Chechen militants killed, various estimates put the number at about 3,000 to over 15,000 deaths. Various figures estimate the number of civilian deaths at between 30,000 and 100,000 killed and possibly over 200,000 injured, Over 500,000 people were displaced by the conflict, which left many cities and villages across the republic in ruins. It also sowed the seeds of deep resentment together with an overwhelming desire to seek revenge.

The town of Beslan is in many ways unremarkable. Lying 900 miles south of Moscow the community is mainly agricultural and industry largely centered on a large vodka-producing factory, far from the pressures of politics and warfare, Beslan had its own life, a mixture of smuggling and other activities that would give Agatha Christi a wealth of material to work with. It was to this town on September 1st 2004, that a group of terrorists from Chechnya came to bring death and destruction, to the magnitude of those during the attacks of 9/11. The target of these men was not military or even a civilian airport.

Compulsion To Kill

They headed straight for Beslan middle school, where parents and children had gathered for the traditional first day of term, the Day of Knowledge. The town had a population of just over 40,000 and several thousand were at the school, students, teachers, grandparents, and onlookers. Although Russian intelligence had received vague reports of a possible attack, in the region, no specifics had been made and therefore one solitary soldier stood guard, as a Russian troop carrier and 3 other vehicles pulled up outside the school. Among the towns people on the ground outside, 49 other terrorists waited and watched. They were the eyes and ears of the assault team.

At a given moment, armed terrorists leapt from the vehicles armed with AK-47 semi automatic rifles, grenades, sniper rifles and explosives. They were immediately engaged by the armed guard, and a police officer in the crowd who drew his sidearm. Both men fired, killing one terrorist before being cut down by a hail of gunfire. With all opposition disposed of, the terrorists then surrounded the crowd, forcing them at gunpoint into the school and eventually into the school gymnasium, into two groups. About 40 % of the crowd managed to break free from the gunmen and escape, the rest were herded inside and the doors barricaded. By 9:05 a.m. the school was surrounded. Inside, up to 50 fanatical terrorists were holding 1,181 hostages, most of whom were children.

Compulsion To Kill

The crowd was stunned and could not understand what was happening and why. One father approached the school to ask and to ascertain the condition of the children. The terrorists immediately shot him dead, dragging his body inside. Such examples were the norm in the first few minutes of the siege. One man inside the building tried to calm the children and restore calm; this was the last thing the terrorists wanted. One walked up to him, put a gun to his head, and executed him in front of the screaming children.

Almost immediately the terrorists began the murder and rape, which was to categorize this incident. Hostages were shot at random while the killers stripped and raped some girls in front of the hostages. Others were taken upstairs and repeatedly assaulted.

As the screaming and gunfire intensified, those outside the school could not have imagined the scenes of horror and cruelty taking place inside. Calls went out for military assistance and in particular to two elite anti terrorist units' code named Alpha and Vympel, were dispatched. These brave men would play a pivotal role in ending the siege, many paying the ultimate price for doing so.

Inside the school the situation became grimmer by the minute. The gunmen had brought explosives and other equipment with them,

Compulsion To Kill

They had also learned from an earlier incident at the Nord-Ost theatre in Moscow and were equipped with gas masks. Explosives were draped around the school and wired up to the hostages. The older children and men were forced at gunpoint to build barricades against the expected assault from the Russian forces. When the barricades were complete the older children and men were singled out, lined up against a wall and shot, their bodies being thrown from an upstairs window. The terrorists were aware that in school sieges in Columbine and Virginia Tech, some students had tackled the shooters. To prevent this, they simply removed anyone deemed old or big enough to pose a risk.

Of course, this siege was not carried out for any reason of forcing concessions or entering into negotiations. This was a new type of terrorism. It was designed to spread horror and dread among the population, this strategy, devised by the twisted mind of Osama Bin Laden was clearly illustrated on 9/11.

The terrorists, who attacked the school that day, were not all Chechen, they included Ingush, Arabs, and North Africans, All were Islamic fundamentalists, and among the group were two women wearing explosive suicide vests.

Compulsion To Kill

I feel that the horrific details of the treatment of the children during the siege would be too graphic for me to repeat in this book, and may detract from the core points I am trying to make. However I do heartily recommend the reader to read *"Terror at Beslan" by John Giduck Archangel Group Inc.* This book gives a stark uncompromising view of the background and aftermath of the siege. As well as a minute by minute account of the event.

The surviving hostages reported after the event, that the terrorists had made no attempt to hide their faces and had made it plain they expected to die.

It is now believed, the intention was to prolong the siege as long as possible while killing and torturing children for maximum shock effect. Events took a sudden turn at 1:05 p.m. on day 3, when one of the bombs in the gymnasium suddenly detonated, followed by a second one. The explosions caught both terrorists and hostages by surprise.

But the result was immediate. The Russian troops outside immediately opened fire without direct orders and moved in. They were engaged by terrorists firing from upstairs windows. Specialist sniper teams engaged these gunmen, and armed citizens in the crowd also joined the firefight.

Compulsion To Kill

Specialist team Vympel stormed the school, blowing holes in the walls to avoid triggering booby-trapped doors and windows. Once inside they shepherded children to the holes and out of the building. Terrorists tried to mow them down as they fled across the playground; the terrorists were well planned and well prepared. They had an easy time shooting helpless children, but now they faced a crack team of commandos. Vympel moved rapidly through the classrooms spraying the ceilings of each room with automatic fire and quickly shooting the terrorist's as they cowered under falling debris from the ceilings. As both Vympel and ALPA teams moved through the building, the terrorists tried to fall back and regroup; they were ruthlessly cut down with no attempt at taking prisoners. These troops had seen the slaughter and torture of the children first hand, they were out to ensure that not one terrorist survived. In this, they were totally successful.

It is however likely that some terrorists did escape in the confusion. It is still unknown exactly how many terrorists took part. What is known however the sickening death toll of 338 dead, and 700 wounded, which included 161 children.

Of course Beslan terrorists did make demands as did the 9/11 highjackers.

Compulsion To Kill

But these demands were purely a feint designed to delay any counter offensive while plans were put into effect to kill as many people as possible. This mass murder concept was not immediately realized by the authorities. At Beslan, much time was wasted while various police and military commanders debated and argued as to how to proceed. Should similar disorganization occur in the USA at a similar event the death toll will likely be even higher.

So! Here we have it. The United States faces some stark choices. We know that evil men are out there. They have an agenda to inflict pain and suffering on the American people. They have both the will and the tools to carry out the job.

To the parents and teachers of their victims, it matters little if the gunman is an idealistic terrorist or a mentally disturbed sociopath. In this book, I have presented chilling details of the killers and the crimes they committed. Not being a psychiatrist I have relied on the published papers of some of the countries foremost experts in both Mental Health and counterterrorism.

I do not claim to have discovered all the answers, nor do I expect everyone to agree with my conclusions. I am sure many will remain convinced that tight gun control is the only answer.

Compulsion To Kill

I respectfully disagree, and back that disagreement with data from the Police, F.B.I., and congressional enquiries.

One thing however is crystal clear. If we choose to ignore the problem, bury our children, and continue with our lives, then there will be more Columbines, Virginia Techs, Beslans, and Newtowns.

Compulsion To Kill

Chapter 10

<u>Conclusions</u>

Well! We have looked at the threat facing our schools. Is it real, and just what, if anything can realistically be done to eliminate the threat? Unfortunately the answer is that we are powerless to prevent such attacks in all cases. We can however, take real and effective measures to minimize the threats.

Schools should never be places we need to imprison our kids. Children, by their very nature are inquisitive and trusting. They do not see right and wrong, good or evil. They see no problem in telling the truth when asked a question, unless they feel they may have done something wrong. Quite simply, at 6 to 9 years they have not yet learned to lie.

Police officers are aware of this and often get useful information as to the perpetrators of a crime, just by listening to children and asking them what they saw. Of course legal restraints prevent them using such evidence in court and once parents or lawyers get involved the kids usually stop talking freely.

Compulsion To Kill

As such, following a school shooting the children are often great sources of information, especially when they have survived when adults or older children may not have.

So! As we have seen, to prevent a school-shooting happening, we need to be on the scene, prepared and alert. This means that we now have to look seriously at having armed security in our school system. This idea will fill the more liberal lawmakers with horror. This is because most people who have no contact with guns see them only as instruments of death. They point to the killings carried out with them and, understandably, wish to keep guns and children as far apart as possible.

This Gun Free Zones idea has not kept our children safe, as Israel found out on May 15th 1974, in the town of Ma'alot and the Netiv Meir Elementary school that was the scene of another mass shooting of school children. The schools were unprotected. The Israeli security attended the scene and initially held back in an attempt to try and negotiate with the three terrorists. This was quickly abandoned when the terrorists began shooting the children.

Israel tried the gun free zone experiment and it failed. America has yet to learn the same lessons.

Compulsion To Kill

In December, The Moorfield Storey Institute, a non-profit educational and charitable organization dedicated to the expansion of social freedom, tolerance, and equality of rights before the law, published a report based on a survey of gun crime in 170 different countries. Initially published in the UK's Guardian newspaper, the report is reproduced below.

"Data shows the United States has 88.8 guns for every 100 people, with a firearm homicide rate by firearm of 2.97 per 100,000 people. The unspoken theory is that reduced ownership of firearms results in fewer murders by firearms—whether it results in more murders by other means is not addressed. (Note: all gun ownership numbers are per 100 people, while homicide rates are per 100,000.)

How does gun ownership correlate with murder by firearms internationally? Argentina is at 3.02, with only 10.2 firearms per 100. The Bahamas has gun ownership of only 5.3, but has 15.37 firearm homicides. Bangladesh has gun ownership below 0.5, yet their death rate by firearms is still 1.1. In Barbados, gun ownership is only 7.8, but the homicide rate is 2.99. In Belize there is only 1 firearm for every ten people, yet the firearm homicide rate is 21.82.

Canada has a relatively high fire ownership rate (30.8), yet a low death-by-firearm rate (0.51). Chile has 10.7 weapons per 100 people, yet a firearm homicide rate of 2.16 per 100,000. Colombia has only 5.9 guns per 100 people, yet the firearm homicide rate is 27.09. Costa Rica has a firearm homicide rate of 4.59, well above the US, but a gun ownership rate of 9.9 per 100, well below the US.

Compulsion To Kill

Croatia and Cyprus have relatively high gun ownership rates (21.7 and 36.4 respectively), but relatively low firearm homicide rates: 0.39 and 0.46.

Ecuador has an ownership rate of just 1.3, but the firearm homicide rate is more than four times higher than the United States;—12.73. In El Salvador the ownership rate is just 5.8, but the firearm homicide rate is 39.9. Finland and France both have relatively high gun ownership rates by international standards, and very low firearm homicide rates: 0.45 and 0.06. Ditto for Germany with 30.3 firearms per 100, but a firearm homicide rate of 0.19.The same is true for Greece with 22.5, but 0.26 firearm homicides.

New Zealand has a firearm ownership rate of 22.6 per 100, but the homicide rate is only 0.16. In contrast, Nicaragua has only 7.7 guns per 100, yet the firearm homicide rate is 5.92. In Norway, 31.3 weapons per 100 people are in private hands, yet the homicide rate by firearms is just 0.05. Panama has a firearm ownership rate well below the US, 21.7%, but a homicide rate well above the US; 16.18. In Serbia, 37.8 people per 100 have a firearm, but the homicide rate is 0.46. South Africa has only 12.7 guns per 100 people but 17.03 is the firearm homicide rate. Sweden and Switzerland have relatively high gun ownership rates—31.6 and 45.7—and have relatively low firearm homicide rates—0.41 and 0.77."

The Guardian's report is skewed, because it only looks at homicides by firearms, instead of total homicides from all causes. We see that some nations have very low rates of gun ownership, yet high rates of murder by firearm. Other countries have relatively high rates of gun ownership, yet very low rates of firearm related homicides.

Compulsion To Kill

So, how do_International Homicide rates from all causes, compare with the presence of guns? I took the numbers the Guardian published, regarding the presence of guns in a society and compared them to homicide rates per country. When I combined the two lists I had data for 169 nations.

The 10 nations with the highest number of privately-owned guns averaged 44.14 firearms per 100 population. Their homicide rate per 100,000 population averaged 2.41. The 10 nations with lowest firearm ownership rates had only 0.44 firearms per 100 population but their homicide rate was 8.96. While the top 10 gun-owning countries have ownership rates 10 times higher than the 10 least armed nations, their homicide rate is 4 times lower. Out of the 169 nations surveyed here, the United States is first in gun ownership, but 86 of these nations have homicides rates higher than the United States.

I then looked at the 25 nations with the highest ownership of guns, versus the 25 with the lowest. The top 25 nations had 33.47 weapons per 100 people with a homicide rate of 1.7 per 100,000 people. The 25 least-armed nations had 0.64 guns per 100 people with a homicide rate of 10.45— more than five times as deadly as the 25 nations with the most guns.

Next, I looked at the 50 nations with the highest number of guns in comparison with the 50 with the lowest. The top 50 averaged 24.79 weapons, with a homicide rate of 5.88. In comparison, the 50 least-armed nations averaged 1.01 firearms per 100 with a homicide rate of 12.17—still more than double their more heavily armed counterparts.

Compulsion To Kill

I then looked at nations with 40 or more guns per 100 people. There are 4 such countries (US, Switzerland, Finland, and Yemen). They average 58.64 firearms per 100 people, with an average homicide rate of 2.85.

Next I took all nations in 30-39% range of gun ownership. There are 12 such nations with an average ownership rate of 32.59 per 100, and an average homicide rate of just 1.48 per 100,000. A further 11 nations have gun ownership rates between 20-29%; their average homicide rate is 3.39. There are 34 nations with between 10 and 19 guns per 100 people; averaging 14.2 guns per 100 with a homicide rate of 9.9. 108 nations have gun ownership rates below 10 per 100 people, averaging 3.53 firearms per 100, they also average 12.92 homicides per 100,000.

The trend seems to be that nations with lower homicide rates have a higher proliferation of guns—the reverse of what is often claimed in the media.

We can also come at this by viewing homicide rates first. The 10 nations with the highest homicide rates in the world, averaging 50.67 per 100,000, have 6.84 guns per 100 people. The ten nations with the lowest homicide rates—just 0.5 per 100,000—have gun rates of 20.39 per 100 people. While the "armed" nations have more than triple the number of privately-held firearms, their homicides rates are just 1/100th those found in the 10 least-armed nations.

Compulsion To Kill

The 25 most deadly nations—with an average of 39.88 homicides per 100,000—have a gun proliferation rate 4.89 per 100. The 25 least deadly nations —0.77 per 100,000— have guns rates of 17.43 per 100.

While it would be stupid to say that gun ownership is the only factor influencing homicide rates, it would be even more stupid to claim that the numbers show that gun ownership increases homicides. The evidence does NOT support that when we look at international data."

Moorfield Storey Institute December 2012

This study is important because it is not done by an anti or pro-gun group. While it correctly concludes that the study does not prove, that gun ownership is not the only factor in crime, it does point out that the evidence does not support tighter restriction on gun ownership. In fact, it concludes quite the opposite. Crime is an unfortunate fact of life. There will always be criminals who will prey on the weaker members of society, just as there will always be politicians who seek to use such tragedies for political ends. In the end, what happens if you or a loved one comes face to face with an armed killer? Noted criminologist Loren W. Christensen, has interviewed hundreds of police officers following deadly force encounters. He describes one such account given by an officer involved in a shooting incident, in his excellent book, 'Deadly Force Encounters.'

Compulsion To Kill

"I focused on the weapon pointed at my face from 12 feet away, and I could see the bullets in the cylinder of the revolver. I saw the suspects forearm muscles and tendon tense as he squeezed the gun. I looked down the barrel and knew I was going to get shot somewhere between my nose and neck, probably my teeth. I fired one shot and it struck the suspect. I couldn't believe I got a shot off before he did."

This stark account from an unnamed officer gives us an insight into the feelings that run through a victims mind. Tunnel vision enhanced visual perception and the realization that death is imminent. This encounter ended not with the death of the officer, but that of the perpetrator.
I am absolutely in favor of leaving no stone unturned in an effort to unravel the psychological makeup of the would-be killer, and of restraints on the availability of violent video games to young and impressionable children.

But at the moment, all other efforts have failed and you as a Mother, Father, Cop or Teacher, are looking down the barrel of a crazed killers gun. Your gun and the ability to use it will be all that keeps you alive. As a certified instructor and permit holder, I carry a gun daily. It is an awesome responsibility, which I do not take lightly. I also stress that responsibility upon those I teach.

Compulsion To Kill

Like all of my students, I earnestly hope that I will never have to use it.

However, if I do, I hope my training and mindset will enable me to prevail and save lives.
Ultimately, the only thing that can stop a bad man with a gun, when they have ignored the laws and security and are standing in front of their intended victim, is a good man (or woman) with a gun.

Disarming the good and hoping that the bad will also put away their guns is a dangerous assumption, one that has been proved false, time and time again, in our so-called gun free zones.
We all need to put aside our political party affiliations and pre- determined dogmas.
We need to decide how we will deal with the mentally ill, and balance that with their constitutional rights. The young and vulnerable in our society deserve our attention and protection.
We owe them nothing less than our unequivocal support.

Stephen Challis *   December 2012

Compulsion To Kill

Compulsion To Kill

Bibliography

The author wishes to acknowledge the following whose published works and papers made this book possible.

- *The Dunblane massacre By Rachal Bell. Neil Kaye, MD Jefferson Medical College in Philadelphia.*

- *M.J. "Monty" Ellsworth, 'The Bath school Massacre.'*

- *Professor Park Elliott Dietz.*

- *Professor Paul Mullen.*

- *Sergeant William O Brien, Aramoana Police Dept New Zealand.*

- *Grant Duwe of the Minnesota Department of Corrections.*

- *The Newgate Calendar.*

- *Professor N. G. Berrill, a forensic psychologist at John Jay College of Criminal Justice in New York City.*

- *Mark Potok spokesman and director of publications and information for the Southern Poverty Law Centre in Montgomery Alabama.*

- *Dr Vaughn Bell. Dr Seena Fazel.*

- *Professor Mark Heyrman, a lecturer at the University of Chicago's Law school.*

Compulsion To Kill

- *Debarred the Use of Arms. (Outskirts Press).*

- *Dr Lynn Fenton a Psychiatrist working for the University of Colorado,*

- *FBI Crime stats 2011.*

- *National Institute of Mental Health.*

- *Psychologists L. Rowell Huesmann and Leonard Eron.*

- *Lt Col Dave Grossman US Army (Rtd) On Combat, Worrier Press.*

- *Terror at Beslan by John Giduck Archangel Group Inc.*

- *Grant Duwe of the Minnesota Department of Corrections,*
- *The Moorfield Storey Institute,*

www.ingramcontent.com/pod-product-compliance
Lightning Source LLC
Chambersburg PA
CBHW070649290526
45790CB00001B/240